HEROES OF HISTORY

THEODORE ROOSEVELT

An American Original

HEROES OF HISTORY

THEODORE ROOSEVELT

An American Original

JANET & GEOFF BENGE

Emerald Books
P.O. BOX 635, LYNNWOOD, WA 98046

Emerald Books are distributed through YWAM Publishing. For a full list of titles, including other great biographies, visit our website at www.ywampublishing.com or call 1-800-922-2143.

Theodore Roosevelt: An American Original

Published by Emerald Books
P.O. Box 635
Lynnwood, Washington 98046

Library of Congress Cataloging-in-Publication Data

Benge, Janet, 1958–
Theodore Roosevelt : an American original / by Janet and Geoff Benge.
p. cm. — (Heroes of history)
Includes bibliographical references.
ISBN 1-932096-10-8
1. Roosevelt, Theodore, 1858–1919—Juvenile literature. 2. Presidents—United States—Biography—Juvenile literature.
I. Benge, Geoff, 1954– II. Title.
E757.B465 2004
973.91'1'092—dc22 2004019799

ISBN-13: 978-1-932096-10-1
ISBN-10: 1-932096-10-8

Fourth printing 2025

Printed in the United States of America

HEROES OF HISTORY

Abraham Lincoln
Alan Shepard
Ben Carson
Benjamin Franklin
Benjamin Rush
Billy Graham
Captain John Smith
Christopher Columbus
Clara Barton
Davy Crockett
Daniel Boone
Douglas MacArthur
Dwight Eisenhower
Elizabeth Fry
Ernest Shackleton
Frederick Douglass
George Washington
George Washington Carver
Harriet Tubman
John Adams
Laura Ingalls Wilder
Louis Zamperini
Meriwether Lewis
Milton Hershey
Orville Wright
Ronald Reagan
Theodore Roosevelt
Thomas Edison
William Bradford
William Penn
William Wilberforce
Winston Churhill

Available in paperback, e-book, and audiobook formats.
Curriculum Guides are available for all of the U.S. biographies.
www.Heroesofhistory.com

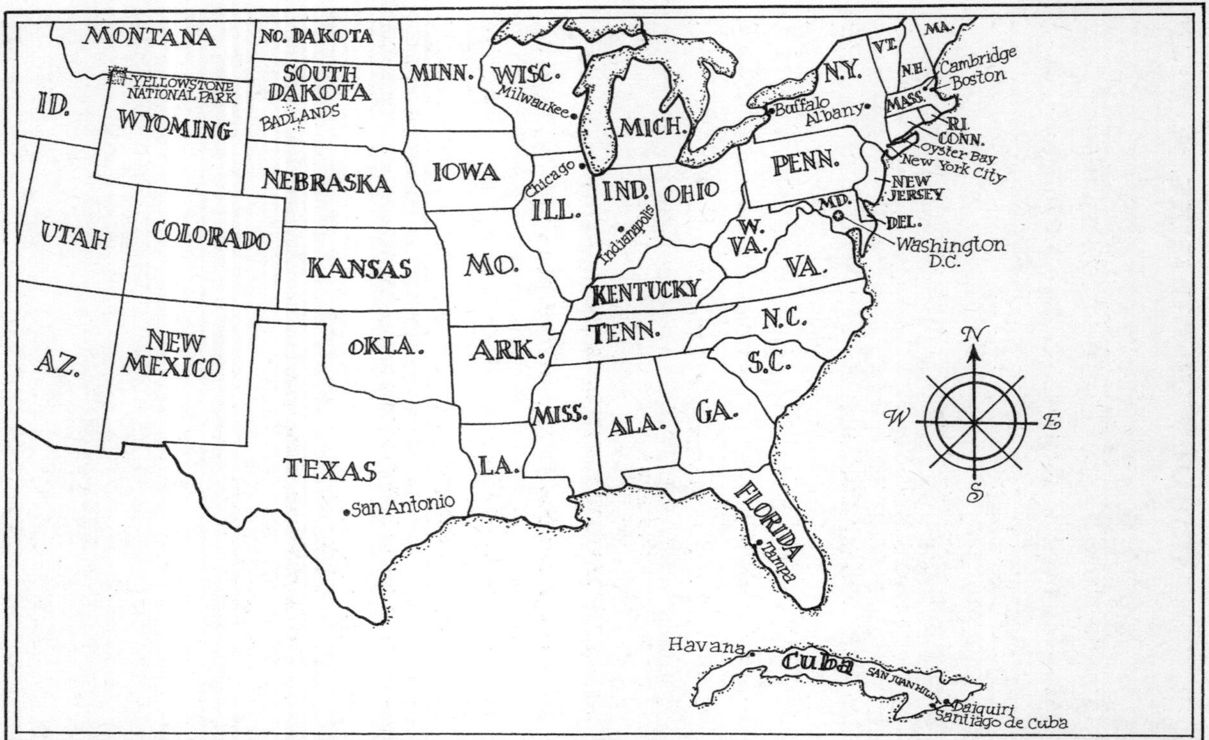
MONTANA
NO. DAKOTA
SOUTH DAKOTA
BADLANDS
MINN.
WISC.
Milwaukee
MICH.
N.Y.
VT.
N.H.
MA.
Cambridge
Boston
MASS.
Buffalo
Albany
R.I.
CONN.
Oyster Bay
New York City
NEW JERSEY
ID.
YELLOWSTONE NATIONAL PARK
WYOMING
NEBRASKA
IOWA
Chicago
ILL.
IND.
Indianapolis
OHIO
PENN.
MD.
DEL.
Washington D.C.
UTAH
COLORADO
KANSAS
MO.
W. VA.
VA.
KENTUCKY
TENN.
N.C.
S.C.
AZ.
NEW MEXICO
OKLA.
ARK.
MISS.
ALA.
GA.
TEXAS
San Antonio
LA.
FLORIDA
Tampa
N
W
E
S
Havana
Cuba
SAN JUAN HILL
Daiquiri
Santiago de Cuba

Contents

Chapter 1

On the Slope of San Juan Hill

Colonel Teddy Roosevelt charged up the slope of San Juan Hill on the island of Cuba as fast as his legs would carry him. Beside him were his men—the First Volunteer Cavalry—and men from other U.S. army units.

The air was thick with bullets fired by the Spanish troops dug in at the crest of the hill. The bullets pelted the ground around Teddy's feet, throwing puffs of dirt into the air, but Teddy kept running. The crest of the hill was in clear sight now. Like the rest of his men, Teddy let out a blood-curdling scream as he rushed forward. Around him men fell to the ground, victims of the bullets the Spanish soldiers fired at them from their powerful German Mauser rifles. Still the men kept running, jumping over the bodies of their dead and wounded comrades.

The Spanish soldiers kept up their furious barrage of gunfire at the approaching Americans, but they could not stem the flow of uniformed soldiers racing up the hill toward them. Outnumbered and overwhelmed, the Spanish troops finally fled toward Santiago, a mile away, leaving the hill to the Americans.

Teddy and his men arrived at the top of the hill to find a number of Spanish soldiers still in position. With his pistol drawn and firing wildly, Teddy leaped into the trenches, and within minutes the remaining Spanish soldiers were dead. The Battle of San Juan Hill was over.

Teddy breathed a sigh of relief. He was tired and battle sore, but he was invigorated and very glad to be alive. His eyes gleamed behind his gold-rimmed spectacles as he surveyed the battlefield. He was proud of how well the First Volunteer Cavalry had fought. The men had suffered heavy casualties, but they had kept advancing. Teddy also had a great sense of personal accomplishment. He was thirty-nine years old, and he had welcomed the opportunity to fight so that he could test himself and his men. And here, on the slope of San Juan Hill, that is what he had done. He had shown immense bravery in the face of the enemy, risking his own life for what he was sure was a noble cause.

Throughout his childhood Teddy had heard the heroic stories of soldiers who had fought in the Civil War. Now he had been in battle himself.

Teddy wished his father could have lived to see this day. How he missed the man. As sweat dripped from his brow and ran down his cheeks, Teddy realized that his father had always believed in him, even when there seemed little hope that the weak, asthmatic child he had been would ever make anything of himself.

Chapter 2

A Southern Outpost

Five-year-old Teddy Roosevelt sat quietly beside his mother, staring at the pale blue walls of the parlor. He hoped that she would forget he was there. The conversation was just getting exciting, to the stage where Teddy was normally sent upstairs to the nursery. However, Teddy's mother, Mittie Roosevelt, seemed too distracted to notice her older son. Instead she turned to her sister. "Anna, read the letter, please. I can hardly bear to wait another moment. We haven't heard from James in months."

Anna unfolded a piece of paper and read, "Dear Mama, Anna and Mittie, I know you will be interested in the following article, which I have copied out in part for you. I do not know if you have heard news from Irvine, but I hear from reliable sources that he escaped harm and is seeking passage back from Europe. It seems, from all accounts, that he had the distinction of firing the last gun discharged from the *Alabama*'s batteries."

Teddy's grandmother, Martha Bulloch, clapped her hands to her face. "Read the article, please," she requested, her voice high with excitement.

Aunt Anna began, "On June 12th 1864, the CSS *Alabama* had the misfortune to be attacked by the USS *Kearsarge* off the coast of France. Although Captain Raphael Seemes and his crew fought bravely, the *Alabama* took a mortal shell to the deck and sank within minutes."

She skipped a passage and continued. "In its short but illustrious career, the CSS *Alabama* captured or sank 69 enemy vessels."

"Thank God Irvine's safe," Martha interjected. "He served the *Alabama* until her last shot was fired! Imagine it, girls. That's what we have to focus on—all the victories the *Alabama* had. I've heard that Lincoln says the war would be over now if the British had not allowed the *Alabama* to be built in their shipyard. And to think that your brother James was the Confederate admiral who was picked to oversee the entire process of construction and take her out to sea, and your brother Irvine was the midshipman who defended her to the last. I tell you, I could not be more proud if I were Robert E. Lee's mother. We'll defeat the Yankees yet! One thing is for sure. I would rather be buried in a pauper's grave than ever have to live under Yankee rule."

"Hush down a little, Mama," Teddy's mother interrupted. "You never know what the servants will repeat."

Martha nodded and then went right on talking. "Things do not look good at the moment with the defeat of the two forts in Mobile Bay. But we will turn it around. The South will prevail!"

As they conversed, Teddy's mother, grandmother, and aunt rolled strips of cotton fabric into bandages. Teddy's heart thrilled every time he thought about the journey these bandages would take, from where he lived on Manhattan Island in New York City, New York, a Union state, to Nassau in the Bahamas, and then through the Union blockade of the South to Roswell, Georgia, in the heart of the Confederacy. His mother and aunt would package the bandages up with toothbrushes, woolen socks, scarves, and soap and hand them to a mysterious messenger who arrived at their front door at number 28 East 20th Street promptly at 9 A.M. every Friday. The package would be passed from hand to hand and would travel by train, wagon, and ship before it arrived in the Bahamas, where it would be off-loaded and reloaded onto a ship bound for the Confederate South. Once it arrived in the South, one of Teddy's mother's relatives—and she had so many relatives that he could not remember half their names—would unpack it and use the contents to help Southern soldiers. These were the exact same soldiers that Teddy's father wished would be defeated by Union troops, for unlike Teddy's mother, who supported the Confederacy, Teddy's father supported the Union.

This was all a bit complicated for Teddy to understand, but the thought of war and blockades and his uncles' escapades on board Confederate ships fired his imagination. In fact, now that his older sister Bamie's spinal condition was a lot better and she did not have to wear a horrible back brace all the time, the two of them would play exciting war games in the local park. Despite his admiration for his southern relatives, Teddy always wanted to play a Union captain routing Bamie, who would be a Southern spy or sometimes a blockade runner.

Although their play was about battlefronts far away, Teddy had heard vague stories of how the war had come close to home the year before. In 1863, while the Roosevelt family had been staying at the beach, terrible riots over the draft laws erupted in New York City. Telegraph poles were torn down, buggies were overturned, prisoners escaped, and homes and businesses all over the city were looted. And although no one told Teddy to his face, he did overhear two of the servants recounting how their friend and neighbor Mr. O'Brien had been torn to pieces defending his home against an angry antiwar mob. In the end, President Lincoln had called in four thousand army troops to quell the rioting. And after the incident was over, Teddy noticed visible scars of its ferociousness all over the city. It seemed strange to him that the North was supposed to be fighting the South, and here were Northerners fighting each other. Still, Teddy dared not ask any questions about it, because he realized that his mother and father themselves supported opposite sides in a very dangerous war.

The three Southern women in the Roosevelt house were able to carry on their practical support of the "enemy" because Teddy's father, Theodore, was seldom home. When he was conscripted into the Union army, he, like just about every other rich man in New York, had paid someone one thousand dollars to take his place on the front lines of the fighting. Teddy had once overheard him explain to Uncle Robert that he would have loved to go and fight for President Lincoln's cause but that he could not risk encountering Mittie's brothers on the battlefield. If he were to kill any of them, he did not know how he would face his wife again. However, Thee Roosevelt, as everybody called him, had found a way to serve the soldiers. And although he told his son about it, Teddy found the details hard to follow.

Thee Roosevelt, who wholeheartedly supported the cause of helping homeless children and downtrodden women, was concerned about the effect so many men being away at war was having on their wives and children. Many of the soldiers spent all of their wages on whiskey and tobacco, leaving their families without any income whatsoever. This meant that many families were thrown out onto the streets, homeless and without food. Teddy's father decided that something had to be done about this. He and two of his friends petitioned Congress to pass a bill allowing soldiers to send home part of their wages before they even got their hands on them and were tempted to buy alcohol. At first a number of senators and congressmen thought this was a crazy scheme. They had never heard of anything like it before. But Thee pressed on until the bill, called the Allotment Bill, was finally passed.

Having seen the bill that far, Teddy's father took it upon himself to explain the new scheme to as many Union soldiers as possible. To do this he tirelessly traveled up and down the Union lines and visited numerous training camps, where he held rallies and urged the soldiers to think of their families and to sign up to send money home. He was getting the message across, but it took a lot of time and effort, which is why Teddy seldom saw him and why Teddy's mother, Aunt Anna, and Grandma Bulloch were able to turn the Roosevelt home in New York into a Southern supply outpost.

Teddy sat quietly as his grandmother talked on. "Not that I am saying anything against Thee," she said, referring to Teddy's father. "He is as loyal and dutiful a man as ever I have seen; he's just on the wrong side, that's all."

Mittie agreed. "I try not to mention the war in my letters to Thee, and I know he tries not to as well. There is no way we are going to sway each other. He simply doesn't understand southern ways."

Grandma Bulloch nodded.

"Still," Teddy's mother continued, "I do find it impossible to be around his entire family when they start up with their views. I hate to ignore the Saturday-night get-togethers, but I can't bear to hear the way they talk about the South." At this point Mittie noticed her son beside her. "Oh, I forgot you were there!" she exclaimed. "Why don't you go upstairs and get David Livingstone's book. I'll come up in a few minutes and read a chapter of it to you."

Even though it would mean leaving the conversation, Teddy left eagerly. There was nothing more exciting than *Livingstone's Missionary Travels and Researches in Southern Africa.* The book was full of fascinating pictures: a herd of galloping zebras, a hugely magnified tsetse fly, and an elephant squirting water through its upturned trunk.

Five minutes later Teddy was happily sitting in his red velvet chair, lost in the book. When his mother finally arrived in his room, he had a lot of questions for her regarding the war. He knew that the War Between the States had begun in 1861, when he was two and a half years old. He could not remember living in peacetime. It seemed perfectly normal to him to see soldiers in uniform in the streets and to listen to adults talk of casualties, victories, and defeats. Still, the war and his family's divided loyalties were terribly confusing. Teddy's mother answered his questions as best she could and then read to her son until his bedtime.

When his mother had left the room, Teddy lay in bed, his mind drifting between the war and Livingstone's fascinating adventures. It was with thoughts of African animals that he finally fell asleep.

The next morning Teddy awoke to the raucous sound of a peacock, and for a long moment he lay with his eyes shut, pretending he was in a campsite on the Zambezi River. The peacock, however, along with a monkey, lived right next door with his Uncle Robert and Aunt Lizzy. Teddy's grandfather, a rich glass manufacturer named Cornelius van

Schaack Roosevelt, or CVS, as just about everyone called him for short, had given two of his five sons, Theodore and Robert, adjoining terraced brownstone houses as wedding presents.

Teddy loved living next to his aunt and uncle. Aunt Lizzy, in particular, shared his fascination with animals. Teddy would never forget the day she led a cow through her living room and down the hall to the back garden. The neighbors in the house on the other side had protested so much about the cow in the backyard that Aunt Lizzy finally had to get rid of it. But during the time it was there, Teddy went over each morning and watched his aunt milk the animal.

As Teddy lay in bed, he heard another sound—a booming laugh. It could belong to only one person—his father. In one bound Teddy was out of bed and dressing himself in his playsuit. Then he ran down the stairs two at a time into his father's arms. But the effort winded Teddy. Running and jumping had winded him a lot lately, and he saw his mother and father exchange worried looks.

Still, Teddy had more important things to think about than a silly asthma attack, and he climbed onto his father's knee and put his head on his father's barrel chest. His three-year-old sister Corinne, whom everyone called Conie, was next to appear, along with her nursemaid. Then Bamie limped downstairs bringing two-year-old Elliot with her. All four Roosevelt children happily munched on buttermilk biscuits and glowed in their father's presence.

Throughout that day Teddy sat spellbound as his father told stories. "And what else?" he kept asking his father, probing for more information about the people he had met on his travels.

The last story Thee Roosevelt told was about his time in Washington, D.C. Thee described how the streets were lined with soldiers, some of whom were even camped out on the White House lawn. He talked of meeting President Lincoln and his son Tad, who was five years older than Teddy. "Tad loves animals, just like you do, Teddy," he said, ruffling his son's hair. "In fact, the only time I saw the president smile was when he told me that Tad had a pony that he rode into the White House and that he even tried to get it to climb the stairs." Then he smiled at Teddy's mother. "And you'll never guess what!" he said. "Mary Lincoln took a liking to me. Once she even asked me to go shopping with her and help pick out some bonnets for her."

Teddy's mother was the first to laugh. "Oh, Thee, she didn't!"

"She most certainly did," Teddy's father replied. "And I think I gave her wonderful fashion advice. You know taffeta bows are all the rage in Washington this spring."

Teddy joined in the laughter as he thought about his burly, six-foot-tall father giving the First Lady fashion tips.

"I shall have to take you with me next time I go to the dressmaker," Teddy's mother teased, "now that I know how sought after you are in the capital city."

That evening several of Teddy's aunts and uncles came to dinner, along with his grandfather. Sometimes the Roosevelt clan spoke in Dutch, which neither Teddy nor his siblings or mother understood. Teddy guessed that they were talking about the war and that they were trying to spare his mother's feelings by not speaking in English.

Finally Teddy's mother shooed the children all off to bed. As he prepared for sleep, Teddy felt another asthma attack coming on. The upstairs servant propped some pillows behind Teddy so that he could try to sleep sitting up, but sleep would not come. By the time the downstairs clock struck midnight, Teddy was gasping for breath. He did not have the energy to go for help, but much to his relief, his father opened the bedroom door and stepped inside.

"Trouble breathing?" he asked.

Teddy wheezed out an answer. "Yes."

The next thing Teddy knew, two big hands were lifting him from the bed. His father held him closely and started walking up and down the hallway, patting his back as he did so. Teddy concentrated on breathing, but it did not get any easier.

"How about a ride?" his father asked.

The thought both terrified and delighted Teddy. A ride with his father was the most daring thing he had ever done. Twenty minutes later the livery servant had harnessed the four horses to the buggy and driven them around to the front of the house.

Teddy's father draped him with a blanket and settled him in the buggy.

"Now hold on," Mr. Roosevelt instructed his son.

Teddy did not need to be told this! He watched as his father took the reins and whipped the horses. Off they rode on a hair-raising gallop through the darkened streets of New York City.

"Breathe deep," Teddy's father yelled as the cold night air rushed past his face.

Teddy followed the instructions, and he felt better as he opened his mouth wide and let the air push into his lungs. The horses kept up their mad dash on the cobbled streets until Teddy's father was satisfied that his son was breathing more easily. Then he turned the horses toward home.

Although Teddy hated to be so sick, he was secretly glad that he could have the time alone with his father. He knew that his father would be staying only a few more days and then would be off again to visit army camps. If only the war were over, Teddy told himself; then he could see Papa every day.

Chapter 3

Living Things

It turned out that Teddy saw his father again soon, though not because the war was over. On October 25, 1864, two days before Teddy's sixth birthday, Grandma Bulloch died after a short illness. Her death took the entire family by surprise, and the Roosevelt household was plunged into mourning. Teddy's father arrived home in time for the funeral, but Teddy noticed that this hardly comforted his mother. Because of the blockades, none of her southern relatives, with the exception of Aunt Anna, who was already in the North, were able to attend. After the funeral service, Grandma Bulloch's body was buried in Brooklyn's Greenwood Cemetery. After her mother was buried, Mittie Roosevelt took to her bed and did not emerge for several weeks.

Meanwhile the war continued to go badly for the South. Soon after Martha Bulloch's death, news reached Teddy's mother that Bulloch Hall, the family's plantation home in Roswell, Georgia, had been ransacked by Union General William Tecumseh Sherman's army as it cut a wide swath of destruction from Tennessee to Savannah, Georgia. Everything of value had been stripped from it, though for some reason the house itself had not been burned to the ground. Teddy heard his mother tell Aunt Anna that she was glad their mother had not lived to hear such a thing.

On April 9, 1865, the War Between the States finally ended. As news of the war's end spread through New York, the residents of the city celebrated by dancing and waving flags in the streets. Five days later, though, the streets were filled with somber-faced people wearing black armbands. The news was shocking but true. President Abraham Lincoln had been assassinated just days after the war ended.

At noon on April 25, the Roosevelt clan, including aunts, uncles, and cousins, gathered at Grandfather Roosevelt's brownstone house on Broadway, at the southwest corner of Union Square. As soon as they could, Teddy and his brother Elliot escaped upstairs to one of the spare bedrooms that overlooked Broadway. A maid named Dora opened the window for them, and they peered down at the huge throng of people below.

"Is that where the procession is going by?" Teddy asked Dora.

Dora nodded with tears flowing down her cheeks. "Stand right there and you should see the casket of Abraham Lincoln. God bless his soul. Take a good look, boys, and never forget it. He be the best man that ever lived."

Teddy was dragging over a stool to stand on when his sister Conie and Edith Carow entered the room. "Papa said we would find you here," Conie said.

Teddy smiled at them. Edith, like Conie, was four years old. She was a shy girl who came to school lessons at the house with Aunt Anna. She had become like a fifth member of the family. Edith even called Aunt Anna Auntie, just like the rest of the Roosevelt children.

The four children positioned themselves on stepstools and stuck their heads out the window. To their left the edge of a black ribbon flapped in the breeze. The ribbon was part of a huge mourning bow the servants had hung from the roof of the house. All the other houses and businesses in the street, along with the gas lamps, also bore signs of mourning.

The children watched as policemen kept the street clear and the procession began to snake its way along beneath the window. A regiment of French soldiers with orange trimmings on their uniforms marched by, followed by several regiments of Union soldiers. Teddy was fascinated to see that many of their dull blue uniforms had holes in them from bullets and pieces of shrapnel. His imagination ran wild as he thought of the battles these men had fought in.

Edith broke into his thoughts. "Where are they all going, Teddy?" she asked.

"Up to Ninth Avenue, to the Hudson River railroad depot," he replied, very proud that he had remembered his father telling him this on the way over.

"Why are they going there?" she asked.

"To put the president's coffin on a train back to Illinois so he can be buried, silly," Teddy replied.

With that Edith started to cry, first with little sobs and then with tears that began to convulse her whole body. "I don't want to see a coffin," she spluttered.

"Then don't," Teddy said forcefully. He climbed down from the stepstool and grabbed Edith's shoulders. "Come on. I want to see everything without you crying in my ear."

Before she had time to react, Teddy had propelled Edith to an adjoining room, one without a window, and locked her in it. She howled and beat on the door, but Teddy returned to his view at the window, determined that Edith was not going to keep him from taking in every aspect of the scene below.

Finally, after thousands of soldiers had streamed by, the funeral wagon bearing President Lincoln's coffin rolled by. The black ostrich plumes that surrounded the coffin fluttered in the spring breeze.

As the procession passed, Teddy thought of the stories his father had told him about being at the White House and how the president smiled only when his children were around. He wondered how

Tad Lincoln was feeling right then, and what kind of hat Mary Lincoln was wearing today.

When the funeral wagon had passed, Conie let Edith out of the room. Edith's expression was as black as the armbands the children were wearing, but she did not say a thing. For a brief moment Teddy felt sorry for what he had done to her but not sorry enough to apologize.

Just as Teddy had anticipated, life was very different for him once the war had ended. His mother and Aunt Anna were a little happier now, though they still talked often about the war and how badly it had gone for the South. His mother intensely disliked the new president, Andrew Johnson, and would not let anyone talk about him in her presence. But most humiliating of all for her was the fact that two of her brothers, James and Irvine, who had worked so valiantly for the Confederate cause, had been banished to England.

Teddy's father stayed home and resumed his prewar activities, including many things Teddy had had no idea he was involved in. There was New York Orthopedic Hospital, for example. Teddy found out that just before the war his father had started the hospital to help poor children with physical disabilities. His father had been so impressed with the work that Dr. Charles Taylor had done on Bamie's back that he had invited him to be the first director of the hospital.

Teddy's father had many other charity concerns, and with the war over and so many widows and injured veterans needing help, there was much to be done. He worked with the Reverend Charles Loring Brace to found the Children's Aid Society and paid for many homeless children to be taken west to start new lives on farms and in small towns there. He also taught a mission class at Madison Square Presbyterian Church and took a great interest in the YMCA, as well as in Miss Sattery's Night School for Little Italians, where immigrant children were taught to read and write in the evenings.

Thee Roosevelt made sure that Teddy and his three siblings learned about the needs of the poor. He also encouraged them to follow their own interests as well. And Teddy's interests could be summed up in two words—living things. Anything that was alive or had recently died drew Teddy like a magnet. Visitors to the house soon learned to peer into the water pitcher before they poured themselves a drink. One of Mrs. Roosevelt's friends failed to do this and was startled when a baby water snake slithered out of the pitcher and into the glass of water she was pouring from it. And the maid threatened to quit when Teddy tied a snapping turtle to the washtub stand and it bit her on the ankle.

Then one day as Teddy was coming home on the streetcar, he met one of his father's friends, Mrs. Hamilton Fish. He absentmindedly lifted his hat to greet her, setting several frogs free from under the hat in the process. Mrs. Fish and several of the other passengers shrieked as they hopped about the streetcar trying to avoid the frogs. When Teddy's mother heard about the incident, she decided to get a little stricter with her son about his animals. She threw out a litter of field mice that Teddy kept under his bed. When Teddy discovered what she had done, he confronted his mother in tears.

"Oh, the loss to science," he wailed, "the loss to science!"

At this, Mrs. Roosevelt relented and allowed Teddy to continue with his nature studies, seeing the huge importance her young son placed on them.

One morning, when he was nine years old, Teddy was sent to the market to buy strawberries for breakfast. Halfway to the market along Broadway, he spotted a dead seal behind a fish stand. Teddy had never seen such a creature before, and he pulled out a notebook and pencil from his pocket and began sketching it. He begged the fish merchant not to get rid of the seal until he had had a chance to take its measurements.

The following morning Teddy was back at the fish stand with his folding ruler. He measured the seal's girth, length, and snout size as best he could. As he recorded the measurements, Teddy imagined himself to be a famous scientist examining a newly discovered species.

Each morning after that, Teddy eagerly offered to go to the market for his mother, and each time he wrote down more details about the seal. Finally, one week after Teddy had first spotted the seal, the fishmonger disposed of it, but not before he had extracted the creature's skull, which he gave to Teddy to take home.

The seal's skull became Teddy's most prized possession and led to a wonderful new idea. Teddy decided that the skull would be the first item in his own natural history museum. The skull was housed on a bookshelf in the back hallway of the Roosevelt home, and Teddy and two of his cousins spent hours arranging and rearranging the exhibit as it grew.

When Thee Roosevelt became one of a small group of men who founded the American Museum of Natural History, Teddy was inspired to write a natural history of insects. After a great deal of thought, he started it with the words, "All the insects that I write about in this book inhabbit North America. Now and then a friend has told me something about them but mostly I have gained their habbits from ofserv-ation."

Having declared his intentions, Teddy spent many happy days studying everything from lady-bugs to dragonflies. He even expanded his definition of insects so that he could write about birds and lobsters!

In April 1868 Teddy's father and mother and Conie visited Savannah, Georgia. Teddy's mother wrote to tell Teddy about all of the beautiful spring flowers there. Teddy replied to her letter, saying that he would love for her to bring some of them home, especially the "buggie" ones. In the same letter, he also wrote: "I jumped with delight when I found you heard the mocking-bird, get some of its feathers if you can.... In the letter you write me tell me how many curiosities and living things you have got for me."

In another letter to his mother, Teddy wrote: "I have got four mice, two white skined, red eyed velvety creatures, very tame for I let them run all over me, they trie to get down the back of my neck and under my vest, and two brown skined, black eyed, soft as the others but wilder. Lordy and Rosa are the names of the white mice, which are male and female. I keep them in two different cages."

When Thee and Mittie Roosevelt finally arrived home from their visit to Georgia, they gave Teddy a box filled with "natural treasures." Teddy was delighted with all the specimens they had brought him.

The trip to Savannah paved the way for something that Teddy had been dreading. Since the end of the war, his father had been considering taking the entire family on a year-long trip around Europe. Teddy could not bear the thought of leaving his friends and animals behind, and he hoped his father would forget about the idea. But while they were away, Conie had developed asthma as well. She did not get as ill with it as Teddy, but nonetheless Teddy's parents decided it was time they all had a complete change of air. Wednesday, May 12, 1869, was set as the departure date. Teddy soon came to think of that date as the beginning of a long prison sentence. By the time the day finally arrived, he had worked himself into such a state that he could not stop crying. In fact, all three of the younger children wailed as their father and mother and nursemaid Mary Ann guided them aboard the luxury paddle steamer *Scotia.* The vessel was bound for Liverpool, England, and as far as Teddy was concerned, for exile from *everything* he loved.

Chapter 4

"I'll Make My Body"

As a silent protest at being taken away from his home, Teddy refused to join in activities with the other children on board ship. Elliot and Conie made new friends, while Teddy sat facing the endless ocean, rereading copies of his *Our Young Folks* magazines. His father tried to cheer him with stories of his grandmother Roosevelt's ancestors, Quakers who long ago had crossed the Atlantic Ocean to join William Penn in his new colony. But Teddy was in no mood to be distracted.

About three days into the voyage, Teddy did allow himself to talk to another passenger, not a child but an adult named Mr. St. John. Mr. St. John was a sickly old man who spoke barely above a whisper. He was from the West Indies, and Teddy could not resist asking him questions about the plants and animals in those islands. As it turned out, Mr. St. John had a wealth of information and stories about wildlife, and the pair were soon engaged in deep conversation on the aft deck. Once Teddy had Mr. St. John to talk to, the remaining six days of the voyage across the Atlantic Ocean passed quickly.

Finally, on the afternoon of Friday, May 21, the *Scotia* steamed through the Irish Sea. The Roosevelt children took turns peering through their father's telescope. Teddy was excited as he saw signs of civilization come into view—windmills, farmhouses, and best of all, the suspension bridge at Holyhead. By nightfall the ship had sailed into the Mersey River and was preparing to dock at Liverpool.

Suddenly Teddy felt frightened by the uncertainty of what lay ahead. While Elliot and Conie poked their heads through the railing, straining to see their uncles in the crowd on the wharf, Teddy slipped into the salon to read a book. His father found him there and firmly propelled him to his cabin to get his carpetbag so the family could disembark.

On the dock, in a swirl of hugs and handshakes, Teddy was introduced to Uncle Irvine and Uncle James. He watched in dismay as his mother burst into tears, clinging to her brothers as if her life depended on it.

The following day the Roosevelt children were introduced to Aunt Hattie and their three young cousins. Teddy found their southern manners a little too much to bear, and he wrote home to his friend Edith, "Conie and I want you very much to play with, the day after we landed we saw our cousins....I do not think you would like them so much because they kiss so much."

For the next few days, Teddy's mother drank endless cups of tea with her banished relatives. She had not seen her brother James for eight years, and they had much to talk about.

In the meantime Thee Roosevelt took the children on day excursions to the seaside. They waded in the ocean and collected shells. Sometimes they went on long carriage rides into the countryside, where Teddy was delighted by the strange plants, hedgehogs, stoats, weasels, and other animals he had not seen before.

On June 2, 1869, the Roosevelt family set out from Liverpool to see Scotland and the rest of England. Accompanying them was Mary Ann, their American nursemaid, and a newly hired English valet. The group of eight traveled north by train. As they neared Scotland, Mrs. Roosevelt entertained the children with stories of her Scottish ancestry on the Bulloch side of the family.

The story that stirred Teddy's imagination the most was about her grandfather six times removed, a man named Archibald Stobo. A well-known Presbyterian minister in Scotland, Archibald convinced a group of Christians to go with him to start a new colony on the Isthmus of Panama in Central America. Three ships set out from Scotland in 1699, with Archibald, his wife, and their only child, Jean, traveling in the lead vessel. When they arrived in

Panama, they ran into bitter opposition from the natives there and eventually decided to return to Scotland. On the way back, the Stobos's ship stopped in at Charleston to take on water and supplies. The ship anchored just outside the entrance to Charleston Harbor.

When the Presbyterians in the town learned that a minister was onboard, they asked if he would come ashore and preach to them. Accompanied by his wife and daughter, Archibald went ashore to preach to the local congregation. That day, with the Stobo family on land, a hurricane struck, sinking the ship and drowning most of those left on board. Having lost everything he owned when the ship sank, and with no money and no ship on which to return to Scotland, Archibald promptly accepted an invitation to become the resident preacher in Charleston. His daughter, Jean, married James Bulloch, another Scotsman, and the Bulloch family line began in North America.

What fascinated Teddy about the story was that neither he nor any of his relatives would exist if the ship had not sunk in the hurricane or if Archibald Stobo had stayed on in Panama as originally planned.

Teddy's mother's stories were nothing compared to the reality of scrambling around abandoned abbeys and climbing the crumbling turrets of twelfth-century castles. Teddy's heart soared as he stood at the base of a stone effigy of a real crusader who died in 1246. Suddenly the history his Aunt Anna had taught him came to life, and he wished he knew even more about the people who had lived out their lives there centuries before.

On the shores of Loch Katrine, Mr. Roosevelt gave a stirring rendition of *The Lady of the Lake,* a poem by the Scottish poet Sir Walter Scott. Teddy's mother broke down when they visited the poet's tomb, telling the children they were on holy ground.

The damp climate of Scotland aggravated Teddy's asthma, and every so often his family had to alter their plans because of it. Yet for the most part, Teddy was encouraged to join in as much as possible.

When the family arrived in London, Mr. Roosevelt set a hectic pace. They visited the London Zoo and the British Museum five times each. Other excursions included the Tower of London, Westminster Abbey, the Crystal Palace, and Madame Tussaud's Wax Museum. It was such a whirlwind of activities that Teddy hardly had time to digest everything he saw.

When their father allowed them time off, the three younger children went for long romps in Hyde Park. They wore matching navy blue sailor suits with white braiding and red silk ties. Unconcerned about tearing holes in their clothes, the children climbed trees and chased butterflies until they fell into a breathless heap on the ground.

The grand tour continued as the family crossed the English Channel and saw the sights of Holland. Teddy learned that Roosevelt was a Dutch name meaning fields of roses. Despite having a Dutch last name and understanding a few Dutch words,

Teddy came to the conclusion that he was thoroughly American. In fact, he and his father counted up and found that Teddy's was the seventh generation of Roosevelts born on Manhattan Island in New York, and all within two miles of each other.

After a trip to The Hague, the tour continued on through Austria, Germany, France, and Belgium. Teddy spent his eleventh birthday in Cologne, Germany. He wrote in his diary that it was the first birthday he had ever spent in snow, and he felt more homesick than ever, despite receiving a pocket looking glass, a portable writing stand, a compass, and a box of miniature dominoes as birthday presents.

The family spent Christmas in Rome, where they settled in for the winter. Even when it was cold and wet, Thee Roosevelt led the family on excursions to catacombs, temples, and churches. They even climbed Mount Vesuvius, where they stopped halfway up for a snowball fight. Teddy found a small fissure in the ground, and at the bottom of it was the fiery orange glow of molten lava. The children were all awestruck as they peered down into it.

When the winter snow began to thaw, the family was off to Paris for their last seven weeks of sightseeing in Europe. While in Paris, Teddy's parents decided that fifteen-year-old Bamie should stay in France and attend finishing school for a year. They selected a school at Fountainebleau, on the outskirts of Paris. The entire family escorted Bamie to the school, and they all cried as they left her there.

Bamie's staying behind marked the first time that the Roosevelt children had ever been separated, and Teddy was very upset by the whole ordeal. The only thing that cheered him was the thought that their long trip was nearly over.

The family crossed the English Channel once again for a final visit with Teddy's uncles, and then on May 14, 1870, the Roosevelts boarded the *Russia*, which was bound for New York City.

It was almost a year to the day since they had left the United States, and Teddy could not wait to be home again. The voyage back across the Atlantic Ocean took eleven days, and most of that time Teddy spent reading or peering over the bow of the ship looking for signs of the New York skyline. He felt a rush of joy as the *Russia* passed Sandy Hook and steamed into the harbor. "New York, hip hurrah!" he shouted, as the first bowline was thrown to a longshoreman and the ship was tied up at a dock on the Hudson River.

Teddy soon realized that a year was a long time to be away from a busy city like New York. During the time he was gone, work had begun on the colossal towers of the East River Bridge that would connect Manhattan Island with Brooklyn. Better yet, a new experimental passenger subway had opened. On a more personal note, Teddy's Uncle Robert had entered politics and announced his run for Congress on the Tammany ticket. Tammany was a powerful arm of the Democratic party in Manhattan, known for vote fraud and other corrupt practices. Neither Teddy's grandfather nor his father was very impressed by this new development, as Boss Tweed, the leader of the Tammany Hall group, had a reputation for being the most corrupt politician in New York.

Still, Teddy did not concern himself too much about such matters. For his part, he was amazed at how quickly life returned to the routine he loved so much. He and Elliot now had their own private tutor, but their friend Edith still came over to the house to do her lessons with Conie, and the four children continued to play games together. Teddy reread the diaries he wrote while in Europe, but he seldom talked to Edith about the trip. In the time the Roosevelts had been away, Edith's family had fallen on hard times. As far as Teddy could gather from whispered adult conversations, Edith's father was out drinking heavily instead of looking for a job. Teddy sensed that Edith would feel bad if he talked with her about their extravagant trip, and so he did not.

The spring of 1870 passed easily enough, except for the rumors that France was about to go to war with Prussia. Bamie wrote Teddy long and detailed accounts about how she could see French emperor Napoleon III's troops marching past her school windows. Teddy envied her, but Grandfather Roosevelt was concerned that Bamie might get caught up in the fighting, and so he pressured Teddy's parents to have her moved to Liverpool, where the family's Bulloch relatives lived.

Everyone had hoped that the change of air in Europe would cure Teddy's asthma, but his condition was as bad as ever. Finally, after a week of Teddy's keeping his parents up all night with his wheezing, Thee summoned his son into the front room. Teddy knew it was serious because his mother followed him in and shut the door firmly behind them.

"Come here, lad," his father said.

Teddy stood in front of him, staring into his intense blue eyes. "Theodore," his father said, using Teddy's full name, "you have the mind, but you have not the body, and without the help of the body, the mind cannot go as far as it should."

Teddy gulped. His father went on. "You must make your body. It is hard drudgery to make one's body, but I know you will do it."

For a long moment Teddy stood in front of his father until he began to feel determination well up within him. Perhaps he could overcome his asthma if he worked hard enough at it. His puny chest swelled as he replied, "I'll make my body."

They were only four words, but they marked a serious change in Teddy's life. Teddy was enrolled in Woods's Gymnasium and went for lessons there every day. He lifted weights, did push-ups, and swung from the parallel bars. This rendered some results, and soon Teddy asked his parents if he could have his own gymnasium at home. They agreed, and John Woods was employed to design a set of exercise equipment that would help Teddy, Conie, and Elliot to improve their fitness level.

The huge veranda, or piazza, on the second floor was turned into the Roosevelts' private gym.

Teddy's friends marveled that his parents would allow such a thing in their home, but Teddy knew that his whole family was focused on getting him strong and healthy.

The plan worked, to a point. Teddy's chest expanded, and he had less trouble with his asthma. But he remained painfully skinny and uncoordinated. No matter how much he practiced, he still managed to do clumsy things. It was not until a year later that Teddy learned something new about his body that explained some of his clumsiness.

It happened when the Roosevelts were renting a summerhouse at Dobbs Ferry, on the Hudson River. One morning shortly after they arrived, Teddy's father presented him with a gun, a breach-loading, pin-fired rifle. Teddy loved the weapon from the moment he laid eyes on it. There was just one problem—he could not hit a single bird or animal with it. Stranger still, when he lent the rifle to his friends, they were able to down ducks with it with remarkable ease. But as Teddy peered into the blue blur of sky, he could not work out what his friends were aiming at.

A week after he got the new rifle, Teddy was riding into town with his father and Elliot. Elliot read aloud a billboard in the distance, and Teddy realized that he was not able to make out the shapes on the billboard, much less convert them into words. No wonder he couldn't shoot anything: he was extremely nearsighted!

Upon learning this, Thee bought his son a pair of gold-rimmed glasses, and for the first time in his life, Teddy could see clearly. He marveled at all the detail around him that he had been missing. Now, as he peered into the sky, he could see what his friends were aiming at with the rifle.

Not long after he got his glasses, Teddy suffered another asthma attack. This time his parents decided to send him to Moosehead Lake, to see if the change of air there might help his breathing. Teddy was sent there alone by stagecoach. Riding with him in the stagecoach were two other boys about his own age. As the trip progressed, the two boys began to tease Teddy, making the journey miserable for him. The teasing slowly turned to punching, and when Teddy tried to strike back, the boys had a knack for getting out of the way of his punches while landing their own on his body. By the end of the journey, Teddy felt totally humiliated. It was then that he decided to make sure that such a situation never happened to him again. He was going to join what he called the "fellowship of the doers." He was going to exercise twice as hard as he had in the past. He would increase his physical endurance and learn the art of self-defense. When he arrived back home, Teddy told his father about his decision. He even managed to convinced his father to let him learn a new skill—boxing.

Chapter 5

A New Hobby

Teddy threw himself into a range of new physical activities. In all of them, he competed with his brother Elliot. As Teddy's father had agreed, the two boys learned to box from an ex-prizefighter. They both also kept notebooks that they filled with the details of the boxing bouts they fought and the best times for their new athletic activities. In his notebook Teddy called himself Skinny and Elliot Swelly, because everyone thought Elliot was such an outgoing and "swell" young man.

On July 17, 1871, just as the family was preparing to vacation in Oyster Bay on Long Island, the news came that CVS Roosevelt, Teddy's grandfather, had died suddenly. Twelve-year-old Teddy watched silently as his father and uncles were enveloped in a flurry of activity, planning the funeral and settling their father's estate.

Before Teddy had time to adjust to the news, the old family home on Union Square was sold and torn down to make way for a new sewing machine factory.

When Teddy's grandfather's money was finally divided up, Thee Roosevelt received over a million dollars in cash. This was an enormous sum of money, and it meant that no one in the family would ever have to work for a living.

In 1872 Thee Roosevelt was appointed as the American Commissioner for the 1873 Vienna Exposition. The money Thee had inherited from his father meant that he could have his entire family accompany him to Europe for the fair. This time he promised the boys that they would rough it more. Besides attending the Vienna Exposition, they would take a boat trip down the Nile River in Egypt and make a horse trek across the Middle East. Teddy wondered how his delicate mother would cope with such adventures, but he did not mention that to his father. It was all too exciting to question.

In keeping with their new wealth, Teddy's parents decided it was time to move up Manhattan Island. Irish immigrants were pressing closer and closer to East 20th Street. They lived in dirty, overcrowded boardinghouses, and like everyone else who could afford it, the Roosevelts felt it was time to leave the lower east side.

Teddy was very depressed to think that they were moving out of his childhood home. But when his father and Uncle James Roosevelt bought adjoining lots on the south side of 57th Street, just west of Fifth Avenue, Teddy realized that he would have to adjust to the new situation. The plan was for the new house to be built while the family was overseas and for the servants to move everything into it once it was completed. The only thing that Teddy looked forward to in the move was the fact that he would be living only two blocks from Central Park, where he could play and explore.

Teddy barely noticed as the rest of the family prepared for the trip to Europe the following fall, because he had a new hobby—taxidermy, by far his most interesting hobby to date. One day when Teddy was out with his father, he paused in front of a small shop on Broadway. He'd passed the place many times before, stopping to stare at the rare stuffed birds displayed in the shop window, but this time he asked his father, "May we go inside?"

His father laughed. "Of course. I was wondering how long it would be before you asked me to introduce you to John Bell."

"You mean you know the man who does this?" Teddy inquired.

"Why, yes. He often does work for the Natural History Museum. He's an old man now, but in his prime he worked with the great John Audubon, stuffing birds for him."

Teddy's mind reeled as he thought of the wealth of information this Mr. Bell must have at his fingertips.

"In fact," his father continued, "I believe he saved Audubon's life once when he was seconds away from being trampled by a wounded buffalo."

With that piece of information, Mr. Roosevelt pushed open the shop door, and they entered another world. Teddy took a deep breath. The smell was unlike anything he had encountered before, strong and chemical but not unpleasant to him.

In front of them, wearing a black frock coat and seated at a large table, was an elderly man with white hair. Teddy liked him immediately.

"Mr. Bell, I have come to introduce my son Teddy to you," Mr. Roosevelt said, reaching out to shake the old man's hand.

Soon Teddy and Mr. Bell were deep in conversation about a pheasant the old man was halfway through extracting the entrails from. Teddy explained how he had often skinned small animals like mice and squirrels, but he had never known how to stuff an animal. Every aspect of what Mr. Bell did fascinated Teddy, and before he left the musty shop, Teddy made his father promise that he could come back once a week for taxidermy lessons from Mr. Bell.

The arrangement worked out well. Mr. Bell taught Teddy how to remove the entrails of an animal and prepare the animal to be stuffed. He also taught him to respect the chemicals used in the process, especially the arsenic. A few grains of it accidentally swallowed or inhaled could be lethal.

In October the family was ready to depart for its second trip abroad. In addition to his gun, Teddy took with him a bag filled with taxidermy equipment. He could hardly wait to get to the Nile. He had heard that the bird life there was spectacular, and he hoped to catch some birds and stuff them. But before they got to Egypt, the family paid a visit to their Bulloch relatives in Liverpool. When they saw each other again, they kissed and hugged just as much as they had done on the first trip, but this time Teddy was expecting it.

While in Liverpool Teddy went to a local store to buy a pound of arsenic. He was disappointed when the store clerk refused to sell it to him. He explained that he wanted it for use in his taxidermy, but the clerk was unrelenting. He told Teddy that he would sell it to him only if he brought an adult along who could vouch that he was not going to use the arsenic to "commit murder, suicide, or any such dreadful thing." Dismayed that he might not be able to do his hobby for the whole trip overseas, Teddy returned to his uncle's house and was relieved when one of the adults accompanied him to the store.

After visiting with their relatives in Liverpool, the Roosevelt family traveled across Europe to Italy, where they caught a ship that took them to Egypt. At the end of November, they arrived in Cairo. While in Cairo the children and their mother visited various mosques and bazaars and the pyramids. Teddy climbed to the top of the Great Pyramid of Cheops and crawled through the narrow passageway inside the pyramid to the king's chamber.

While his family was sightseeing, Thee went in search of a *dahabeah*, an Egyptian houseboat, to charter for the trip up the Nile River to Aswan. Finally he found the *Aboo Erdan*. The vessel had a small stateroom for each member of the family, a salon and dining room, and a bath. A large awning protected the deck from the hot Egyptian sun. The *Aboo Erdan* had a crew of thirteen, and Thee chartered it for two months.

Before the family left Cairo on December 12 for their trip upriver, Teddy purchased a field guide to the birds of the Nile. He was anxious to identify and stuff as many different species of birds as he could on the trip.

As they moved upriver, they were going against the current and progress was slow. When there was not enough wind to fill the sail and propel the boat forward, the crew would scramble ashore and haul the vessel upriver using long ropes attached to the bow.

Life quickly fell into a leisurely pace for the Roosevelts aboard the *Aboo Erdan*. For two hours each morning, the younger children studied French and other subjects under Bamie's guidance, and then they were free to play and explore. The boat made many stops along the river so that the family could visit the numerous ancient ruins that dotted the riverbank. Teddy loved to climb over these ruins and explore them, but most of all he liked to go after birds. He would identify a particular species of bird and then try to shoot one of them with his rifle. In the evenings he would take the birds he had caught, lay them on clean sheets of paper, and practice his taxidermy skills on them. The Egyptian crew watched in wonderment as he carefully prepared the birds and finally stuffed them with cotton wadding.

Teddy did not seem to notice the smells associated with this process, or the fact that he was beginning to smell much like the birds he was stuffing. He overheard Bamie telling Conie that they should stand upwind of him, but Teddy did not care; he was lost in his own world of animals.

Late in January 1873, the *Aboo Erdan* reached Aswan. After some exploring there, the houseboat turned around and began the journey back to Cairo. The houseboat was traveling with the current now, and so the journey back was much faster than the voyage upriver had been.

From Cairo the family set out on horseback across the desert and into Palestine. They visited Jerusalem, which Teddy thought was much less grand than he had expected, and swam in the Jordan River, which Teddy decided would qualify as only a stream in America. They traveled on through Lebanon, Turkey, and Greece before finally arriving in Vienna, Austria, for the exposition on April 19, 1873.

After traveling on the Nile by boat and across the desert on horseback, Teddy found Vienna a boring place. His father was busy with preparations for the American exhibit at the exhibition, and his mother was preoccupied with Bamie's formal introduction to European society. During his stay in Vienna, Teddy wrote in his journal, "The last few weeks have been spent in the most dreary monotony."

The monotony was finally broken when, in the middle of May, Thee escorted Teddy, Elliot, and Conie to Dresden, Germany, where he had arranged for them to spend five months with a German family learning German.

Dresden was an old city set on the banks of the River Elbe. It was surrounded by hills covered with rows of vines, and beyond the vineyards was lush forest. Teddy liked the place immediately. The children moved in with the Minkwitz family. Hofsrath Minkwitz, a formal but caring man, was a city councilor and member of the German Reichstag. His wife was a rather plump woman who plied the children with cakes and other goodies. The Minkwitzes had three daughters and two sons. The two sons particularly fascinated Teddy. They were both famous fencers. One was nicknamed Der Rothe Herzog (the Red Duke), and the other Herr Nasehorn (Sir Rhinoceros) because the tip of his nose had been cut off during a fencing match and had been sewn back on.

Fräulein Anna, the Minkwitzes' eldest daughter, took charge of teaching the Roosevelt children German and arithmetic. The children were kept busy with their studies, and in a letter to his mother, Teddy laid out their daily schedule for her.

> Halfpast six, up and breakfast which is through at halfpast seven, when we study till nine; repeat till halfpast twelve, have lunch, and study till three, when we take coffee and have till tea (at seven) free. After tea we study till ten, when we go to bed. It is harder than I have ever studied before in my life, but I like it for I really feel that I am making considerable progress.

The Minkwitzes spoke only German in the house, which forced Teddy, Elliot, and Conie to quickly grasp the language to be understood.

While the children were in Dresden, Bamie was spending time in London and Paris with their mother. Teddy wrote a letter to her in which he succinctly took stock of how things were going for him in Dresden.

> My dear darling Bamie,
>
> I wrote a letter on the receipt of yours, but Corinne lost it and so I write this. Health; good. Lessons; good. Play hours; bad. Appetite; good. Accounts; good. Clothes; greasy. Shoes; holey. Hair; more 'a-la-mop' than ever. Nails; dirty, in consequence of having an ink bottle upset over them. Library; beautiful. Museum; so so. Club; splendid.

Teddy did encounter a few difficulties in staying with the Minkwitzes. His hosts confiscated his supply of arsenic, and several mice he was keeping in a bureau drawer were thrown out the window. But seeing Teddy's passion for animals, the Minkwitzes proposed a compromise allowing Teddy to continue collecting specimens from the woods outside Dresden. The Minkwitzes continued to be concerned, though, when snakes and other small critters kept escaping from Teddy's bureau drawers into the house.

About three months into his stay in Dresden, Teddy once again suffered a serious bout of asthma.

When his mother learned that he was again having to sleep sitting up, she traveled to Germany and took the three children to Switzerland, where she hoped the mountain air would help her son's asthma.

After three weeks in the Alps, Teddy's asthma had subsided and Mittie Roosevelt took the children back to Dresden.

"I wonder what will become of my Teddy," Mittie confided to Fräulein Anna before she left the children to return to London.

"You need not be anxious about him," Fräulein Anna said. "He will surely one day be a great professor, or who knows, he may become even president of the United States."

Chapter 6

No Longer Junior

Things were very different when fifteen-year-old Teddy Roosevelt arrived home from Dresden in late autumn 1873. The family moved into the new house on 57th Street, even though it was not quite finished. All of the internal woodwork had been ordered from Pennsylvania, but the order was running behind schedule. Teddy could see that the new house, even in its unfinished state, was much more magnificent than the old home on East 20th Street. It was enormous, with long corridors and fireplaces in most rooms. Glass-fronted bookcases were built into the walls, and large, glittering chandeliers hung from the ceilings.

While the children were away in Dresden, Teddy's father had bought the summerhouse at Oyster Bay on Long Island. The East River Bridge, or Brooklyn Bridge, as it was now called, had finally been completed. That eliminated the need to catch a ferry across the East River on the way to Oyster Bay, making the trip there much faster.

The summerhouse, named Tranquility, was built in a southern style, and Teddy spent the following summer there. The house was anything but tranquil when the Roosevelt children descended upon it. Conie and Elliot were allowed to pass most of their time taking leisurely horseback rides through the country lanes and playing along the shoreline. But Thee and Mittie Roosevelt had other plans for their older son. Now that Teddy was in much better health, they felt he should be preparing for a place at Harvard University, so Teddy passed much of the summer studying.

In the fall, after the family returned to the house on 57th Street, a tutor named Arthur Cutler was engaged to assess Teddy's academic strengths and weaknesses. The results were not surprising. Teddy was far above average in history and geography—mostly, he decided, because of his travels and reading—exceptional in natural history, very good in French and, of course, German, but sadly lacking in mathematics, Greek, and Latin.

Once he knew what Teddy had to work on, Arthur set to work preparing his charge for the entrance examinations to Harvard. It was a serious course of study, and it took up much of Teddy's time. In what little time remained, Teddy's mother organized such things for him as dancing lessons and social picnics with girls.

Teddy had spent most of his life with Bamie and Conie, but when it came to girls outside of his family circle, he did not know what to say to them. Since they were not interested in dissecting animals or boxing matches, he tried to avoid being cornered by them in social situations.

There was one girl, however, with whom Teddy always felt perfectly at ease—Conie's childhood friend Edith Carow. Edith often visited Tranquility, and Teddy enjoyed taking her out on the bay in his rowboat, so much so that he named the boat after her.

As the seasons changed, Teddy continued to study eight hours a day, five days a week, and much to his delight, he passed all eight Harvard entrance exams. He was accepted as a freshman for fall semester 1876.

Having worked so hard to get in, Teddy now had time to think about what attending Harvard would really be like. It did not take him long to get cold feet about the whole idea. He realized that his mother had closely orchestrated his entire social life and that the only other people his age he knew well were his brother, sisters, cousins, and a few longtime friends of the family. The thought of going to college in Cambridge, Massachusetts, and mixing with young men he had never met before daunted him.

Teddy's course was set, however, and on Wednesday, September 27, Teddy's father saw him off from the station at Syosset, Long Island. His father had one piece of advice for him: "Take care of your morals first, your health next, and finally your studies."

Teddy agreed, promising not to smoke or drink liquor and to respect any young ladies he was introduced to.

Following the train ride to Cambridge, Teddy hired a trap to take him to Mrs. Richardson's boardinghouse at 16 Winthrop Street. Bamie had found the place and arranged the furniture for him. As Teddy looked around at the room for the first time, he was confident he could make it home for the next four years.

A month later, on his eighteenth birthday, Teddy wrote home to his family.

> I do not think there is a fellow in College who has a family that loves him as much as you all do me, and I am sure that there is no one who has a father who is also his best and most intimate friend, as you are mine. I have kept the first letter you wrote me and shall do my best to deserve your trust.

As far as his studies were concerned, Teddy reported, "I think I am getting along all right in all."

Teddy was taking classes in Greek, Latin, German, classical literature, mathematics, physics, and chemistry. Natural science, the subject he had been looking forward to the most, was a sophomore class.

As the college's football team was chosen, Teddy looked on enviously. Although he would have loved to play on the team, at five feet eight inches tall and 125 pounds he was far too slight to be considered. Thankfully Harvard had both a boxing and a wrestling team, two sports in which boys of the same weight were pitted against each other. Teddy wrote home for his boxing gloves and headed for the gymnasium, where he was promptly signed up for the lightweight boxing championship. He made it as far as the semifinals, which he considered a personal best.

As they had always done, Greek, Latin, and mathematics stretched Teddy's academic abilities, but Teddy persevered with them.

While Teddy was coming into his own physically and academically at Harvard, Elliot was undergoing a mysterious decline in his health. He had always been the strong, healthy son, and now he was having strange fainting fits that the doctors diagnosed as "congestion of the brain." The fainting fits became so bad that Thee stopped Elliot's studies and took him to England to see if the change of air might do his son some good. But in England Elliot's health got even worse. Shocked at the change in his younger son, Teddy's father wrote to say that he had sent Elliot to Texas in the hope that riding the wide-open range there would restore his health.

Teddy had to admit that except for Elliot's illness, he was jealous of this new, carefree life his brother had. The West was a place of romance and adventure, and Teddy promised himself that somehow he, too, would one day make it out west.

In the meantime Teddy continued to work hard at Harvard, and when the school year ended, he found that he had passed Greek, though barely. But a pass was a pass, and as soon as his first year was over, Teddy and his college friend Harry headed for the Adirondacks in New York State. Like Teddy, Harry had a broad knowledge of birds, especially those found in the northeastern United States. The two young men collected specimens of various birds, observed them in the wild, and wrote lots of notes. They also worked together on a book called *The Summer Birds of the Adirondacks in Franklin County, N.Y.*, in which they catalogued all the birds they had seen. They shared the costs of having the book printed.

Following his stay in the Adirondacks, Teddy went to the house at Oyster Bay with the rest of his family. It was there that he and his father had a serious talk. The United States had been in the grip of an economic depression since the Panic of 1873. With fewer new homes and businesses being built, the demand for plate glass was down. Mr. Roosevelt pointed out to Teddy that several of his cousins were eager and able to carry on the shrinking family business. So there was no need for Teddy to think he had to follow his father and grandfather into the glass manufacturing business.

Teddy was relieved to hear this. He had never been particularly interested in the glass business, and this freed him up to consider a career in science. Science was not a good way to get rich, however, and his father had a piece of advice for

Teddy. "If you are not going to earn money," he said, "you must even things up by not spending it. You have to keep the fraction constant, and if you are not able to increase the numerator, you must reduce the denominator."

Teddy understood perfectly what his father was saying. Thee was a hard worker, and the last thing he wanted was a dilettante for a son, a person who dabbled in science but never made any significant contribution to it.

In truth, Teddy's father was in the middle of a career change himself. For the first time in his life, he had entered the political arena. Thee Roosevelt had come to the attention of President Rutherford Hayes, and the president had nominated him to be the collector of taxes for the Port of New York. It was a huge honor, and one that Teddy's father looked forward to taking up. However, as the summer unfolded, Thee learned that his nomination had rankled New York's powerful Senator Conkling to such an extent that a vicious political fight erupted over his nomination. Teddy was sorry to see this happen and wished his father had stayed out of politics. Before the matter was resolved, it was time for him to return to Harvard.

The second year at college was much more relaxing for Teddy than the first. By now he understood how the system worked, and he had made a few close friends. And the courses were more to his liking. He took zoology, botany, constitutional history, German, and French. The only subject he struggled with was French, but he persevered with it.

Teddy was just getting into the rhythm of school when he received a letter from his father telling him that Senator Conkling had prevailed, blocking his nomination for good. "The machine politicians have shown their colors.... I fear for your future. We cannot stand so corrupt a government for any length of time," Thee wrote.

A week later, when Bamie wrote to tell Teddy that their father was experiencing terrible stomach pains, Teddy blamed the ailment on the stress of the fight over his nomination.

By Christmas, though, Thee appeared to be much better. The house on 57th Street, which was now finished, was filled with the usual array of festive friends and family. The new home was large enough to accommodate five hundred guests at a time, and as usual the Roosevelt Christmas gathering was lavish and well attended. Elliot was back from Texas, feeling better and looking older and weather-beaten. He swaggered like a cowboy and told endless stories about his adventures. All of this kept the family happily occupied, and by the time Teddy returned to Harvard for the spring semester, he was convinced that the family was doing well. That is, until he received several vague letters about his father's feeling ill again. Elliot had taken over the role of nursing him and promised to summon Teddy if matters became any worse.

On Saturday afternoon, February 9, 1878, Teddy was called to his professor's office to receive a telegram. The telegram told him that his father's condition was worsening and he should return to New York immediately.

Teddy ran back to his room at the boarding-house on Winthrop Street and quickly packed some clothes into an overnight bag before heading to the train station, where he caught the night train to New York City. When he arrived in New York the following morning, Teddy found the flags around the city flying at half-staff. He quickly learned that this was in honor of his well-known father, who had died just before midnight.

Teddy was so devastated by the news that he hardly noticed the crowd of rich and poor people who had gathered outside the house on 57th Street to pay their respects to a man who was loved and respected by so many throughout the city for the practical ways in which he had shown charity to others.

Inside the house Teddy tried to console his mother, sisters, and brother, but it was not easy for him. Teddy felt guilty that he had not been there to hug his father good-bye and comfort him in his dying moments.

In his grief Teddy took out his dairy. He drew a thick black line down the margin and then wrote, "My dear Father. Born Sept. 23, 1831." It was not until February 12, two days later, after the funeral, that he could write any more. He dipped his pen into the ink bottle and poured out his bitter feelings.

> He has just been buried. I shall never forget these terrible three days; the hideous suspense of the ride on; the dull, inert sorrow, during which I felt as if I had been

> stunned, or as if part of my life had been taken away, and the two moments of sharp, bitter agony, when I kissed the dear dead face and realized that he would never again on this earth speak to me or greet me with his loving smile, and then when I heard the sound of the first clod dropping on the coffin holding the one I loved dearest on earth. He looked so calm and sweet. I feel that if it were not for the certainty, that as he himself has so often said, "he is not dead but gone before," I should almost perish. With the help of my God I will try to lead such a life as he would have wished.

With the death of his father, Teddy had big shoes to fill, and he knew it. He no longer wrote junior after his name; he was now the only Theodore Roosevelt. People had loved and respected his father, and now Teddy knew that they would be looking to him for that same strength of character that Thee Roosevelt had displayed to all he met. He wondered whether he could ever be as great a man as his father had been.

Chapter 7

Sunshine

Two weeks after Thee Roosevelt's death, Teddy was back studying at Harvard. He could scarcely believe that his father was gone, and he poured out his grief in his journal.

> Have been thinking about Father all evening, have had a good square breakdown, and feel much better for it.
>
> Every now and then there are very bitter moments; if I had very much time to think I believe I should go crazy.
>
> He did everything for me, and I nothing for him. I remember so well how, years ago, when I was a very weak, asthmatic child,

> he used to walk up and down with me in his arms...and oh, how my heart pains me when I think I never was able to do anything for him during his last illness!
>
> I am working pretty hard but I do not care so much for my marks now; what I most valued was his pride in them.

As a way to deal with his grief, Teddy threw himself into his studies. He also went on a shopping spree. Soon after the funeral his Uncle James took him aside and announced that Thee had left Teddy $125,000 in cash. This, Uncle James calculated, meant that if Teddy invested it, he would receive $8,000 a year in interest. Considering that the president of Harvard University lived exceptionally well on a yearly salary of $5,000, this meant that Teddy could have almost anything he wanted.

On his shopping spree he bought new suits and boots in various colors, spending $761 on clothes for himself. Teddy also had his horse Lightfoot brought to Cambridge, and he enjoyed driving around town in a trap drawn by his horse.

Teddy was relieved when summer arrived and he was able to retire to Oyster Bay with the rest of his family. But the summerhouse was filled with constant reminders of his father. Sometimes the memories were too much to bear, and Teddy would saddle up Lightfoot and take long gallops through the countryside.

By late August Teddy was yearning for something different, so his old tutor Arthur Cutler arranged for him to go and trek among the wilds of Aroostook County in northern Maine. Arthur had visited the area before and told Teddy he would enjoy it, as it contained one of the last stands of virgin forest in the Northeast. Bill Sewall, an experienced woodsman who lived in the area, was engaged to be Teddy's guide.

Getting to Island Falls, Maine, where Bill lived, was quite a trip, taking Teddy two full days to arrive there from New York. Two cousins, Emlen and West Roosevelt, accompanied Teddy on the trip. When he got to Island Falls, Teddy liked Bill immediately. Bill, like Teddy, loved poetry and would quote it out loud as they trekked through the woods.

The first day of their trek they covered twenty-six miles, Teddy matching his guide step for step and poem for poem. Along the way they stopped to shoot birds, collect bugs and insects, and examine the varied plant life. But all too soon it was time for Teddy to return to Cambridge, Massachusetts, for another year of study.

Teddy arrived at Harvard for the first day of the new semester with renewed confidence. Unlike most of his eight hundred fellow students, he had pitted himself against the virgin American landscape during the summer and had not only survived but also thrived. Asthmatic or not, he was one of the fittest and most adventure-loving young men in the school, and he was proud of the fact.

Teddy's newfound confidence opened many doors for him. As he described it to his mother in a letter, "Funnily enough, I have enjoyed quite a burst of popularity since I came back." Indeed, clubs vied to have him join, and soon Teddy was a member of the prestigious Porcellian Club, the Hasty Pudding Club, the Rifle Club, the Art Club, the Glee Club, and the Natural History Society.

As if involvement in all these clubs were not enough, within weeks of returning to college, Teddy was introduced to Alice Lee, the seventeen-year-old cousin of Teddy's college friend Dick Saltonstall. Alice's family called her Sunshine, and from the moment he met her, Teddy could see why. Alice was the prettiest girl he had ever laid eyes on. She was tall and willowy and had long honey-blonde hair and sparkling blue eyes.

Teddy found he suddenly had a new and overwhelming focus for his life—to woo and marry Alice Lee. He embarked on his plan with gusto, getting up at six in the morning and studying until lunch. After lunch he would ride Lightfoot the six miles to Chestnut Hill, where Alice lived, and escort her on long walks.

Teddy and Alice would ramble through the countryside, picking up chestnuts, observing squirrels at play, and listening to the various bird songs. It was an idyllic time, and by the spring of 1879, Teddy felt the time was right to propose to Alice. Much to his surprise, she turned him down. But she didn't close the subject off completely, giving Teddy hope that she might one day reconsider his proposal. This hope spurred Teddy on to even greater romantic feats, and finally Alice agreed to marry him.

Now that he was engaged to Alice, Teddy thought less about becoming a natural scientist. To be the best in his field, he would have to study in Europe for two years, and right then two years seemed an interminably long time to postpone his wedding date. In the end he decided to study law in New York City, and October 27, 1880, after Teddy's graduation from Harvard University, was set as the date for the wedding.

Finally his days at Harvard were over, and Teddy graduated with a B.A. *magna cum laude.* He finished twenty-first in a class of 177 students, having done particularly well in political and natural sciences.

Even though Teddy had graduated with honors, a black cloud was hovering over this time. During his last semester at college, Teddy had a routine physical examination by the college doctor. He marched into Dr. Sargeant's office expecting to be told he was in excellent health.

As the doctor examined him, Teddy noticed him grow grim. When he was finished, Dr. Sargeant looked Teddy in the eye. "Mr. Roosevelt," he said, "the news is not good. You have a weak heart. You must refrain from strenuous activity, even running up the stairs. And you must choose a sedentary occupation for yourself. If you do not, you will not live long."

Teddy's mind reeled for a few moments at the news, and then Teddy told Dr. Sargeant bluntly,

"Doctor, I'm going to keep doing all the things you tell me I can't do, even if it means I have a short life. While I'm alive, I'm going to live." With that he stood and left the room, while the doctor sat in stunned silence.

Teddy decided not to tell anyone about the doctor's dire prediction, especially Alice, since there was no way he was going to follow the doctor's advice. In fact, he determined to push his heart even more than normal to prove Dr. Sargeant wrong.

As a graduation treat, Teddy decided that he and Elliot should take a strenuous western hunting trip together. He planned things out in such a way as to incorporate as much physical exercise as possible. The two of them traveled by train through Ohio to Chicago, and from there they took another train on to Iowa. Both Teddy and Elliot knew it was the last time they would be the carefree Skinny and Swelly, and they made the most of every minute of the trip. They spent six weeks hunting and trekking around Iowa, Illinois, and Minnesota. As he hunted, Teddy was impressed by the vastness of the western prairie. He had never seen such big farms, and the expansiveness of the sky and the horizon was unlike anything he had seen before.

As the end of September approached, Teddy and Elliot climbed back on the train for the trip back to New York. It was time for Teddy to start focusing on his wedding, which was now only a month away.

Wednesday October 27, 1880, was Teddy's twenty-second birthday. It was also the day he and

Alice Lee were married in Brookline, Massachusetts. Elliot was best man at the wedding, and Alice's cousin Rose Saltonstall was the maid of honor. Edith Carow, Teddy's boyhood friend, was the only nonfamily member to be invited to the wedding.

Following the service a reception for the couple was held at the Lee estate at Chestnut Hill, and at four in the afternoon the newlyweds departed the reception for Springfield, where they spent the night. The following morning they set out for Oyster Bay, where they spent the next two weeks at the summerhouse.

Teddy loved being married to Alice. She was such a bright, happy person. In the midst of his joy, he couldn't help feeling a little sorry for Bamie. She had turned down the opportunity to marry a distant and much older cousin, James Roosevelt. Instead Bamie had introduced James to her friend Sara Delano, and the two had married just weeks before Teddy and Alice. Teddy expected that that could well be the one and only offer of marriage that Bamie would receive. Her posture was stooped and awkward from her spinal condition, and she looked serious and studious most of the time, two traits that Teddy feared most of his male acquaintances would find unattractive.

The Roosevelt family welcomed Alice with open arms. Not only did she come from one of the best families in Boston, but also she was unerringly polite and sociable. Better still, she seemed to understand how much Teddy meant to his mother and sisters and was ready to share him. This was a good thing, because after their honeymoon at Oyster Bay, the new Mr. and Mrs. Theodore Roosevelt went to live with Mittie, Bamie, and Conie in the Roosevelt home at 6 West 57th Street.

Elliot, being relieved of his duty as the only man in the house, set off for an adventurous trip to Europe and India. He wrote back from England to say that he had enjoyed the voyage across the Atlantic Ocean. By coincidence, James Roosevelt and Sara Delano Roosevelt were aboard the ship as well, taking a delayed honeymoon. Elliot reported that the three of them had gotten along splendidly and that James had even confided in him that Sara was pregnant and the couple would like Elliot to be the child's godfather.

Meanwhile Teddy moved ahead with his education. He enrolled at Columbia Law School, which was quite a letdown after attending Harvard. The school was located in a dingy converted house on Great Jones Street, fifty-four blocks down Fifth Avenue from 57th Street. Teddy walked there each morning, arriving in time for lectures at eight-thirty in the morning. The lectures mostly consisted of a professor dictating detailed notes to the students. It was all Teddy could do to keep up with the pace of the professor's dictation. But he had promised himself that he would study hard, and that is exactly what he did.

In his spare time, Teddy decided to research and write a book on the Naval War of 1812. He worked hard on the project so that he would have something to show his Uncle James Bulloch when he and Alice traveled to Europe the following May. In the meantime something quite different was attracting his attention—politics.

At night, before he and Alice went out for dinner with various wealthy and influential citizens of New York, Teddy, clad in his formal evening clothes, would cross Fifth Avenue, walk north two blocks, and head east on 59th Street until he came to Morton Hall, located above a saloon. Morton Hall housed the Twenty-first District Republican Association, and its name was grander than the large, dingy room filled with spare wooden benches, brass spittoons, and a podium at the front. Lawyers, saloon keepers, storekeepers, and streetcar conductors, among others, gathered in the hall for "bull sessions," during which they discussed politics in the district. At first these men were suspicious of Teddy, dressed in his evening clothes, but Teddy did not care. Despite the less than welcoming atmosphere, Teddy continued to attend the bull sessions, and slowly and begrudgingly the men began to accept him. One of the men, an Irishman named Joe Murray, did his best to befriend Teddy. As Teddy participated in the conversations and listened to what others had to say, a desire to participate more actively in the politics of New York State began to grow within him.

While Bamie and Conie and his mother were supportive of Teddy's new desire, other members of the Roosevelt clan were not so excited about it. Teddy's cousins Alfred and Emlen and his Uncle James Roosevelt tried to discourage him. Local politics, they reminded Teddy, was not for men as refined as he. Low-level politics was full of riffraff and other people of dubious motive, and Teddy's father would not have approved of his being involved in such an enterprise.

Teddy took their words to heart. Although he had a desire to be more involved in New York politics, he was not sure whether he should go ahead and do it. Since he was about to set off on his trip to Europe with Alice, he decided he would mull the whole issue over while he was away.

Chapter 8

Assemblyman

Life has never been better, Teddy told himself as he escorted Alice up the gangplank of the *Celtic*, the steamer that would ferry them to Europe. A day later he was surprised to discover what a poor sailor his new bride was. In fact, as Teddy was to find out soon enough, Alice hardly kept a meal down during the entire nine-day voyage. Teddy was soon exhausted tending to her needs.

Once they reached Ireland, their first port of call, Alice made a speedy recovery. Teddy wrote home that Alice "is the best travelling companion I have ever known." Together they explored the green countryside and marveled at the crumbling monasteries. Only one thing marred Teddy's delight in Ireland—the condition of the poorest people. Scattered across the countryside were windowless, sod hovels inhabited by wide-eyed children who ate only potatoes and whatever scant supply of milk a bony cow could provide. These sights upset Teddy, and at one stage he ordered the carriage driver to stop so he could give ten dollars to a man who was so hungry he had fallen at the side of the road.

From Ireland they traveled on to Liverpool, where they were greeted by an entirely different scene. Teddy's Bulloch uncles, aunts, and cousins were all waiting eagerly to meet Alice and welcome her into the family. Teddy loved being with his relatives, but he acknowledged in a letter to his mother that they had retained many of their southern ways, despite having lived in England for nearly eighteen years. He also pointed out to his mother that there was still "the everlasting slobbering (there is no other word for it) of the younger Bullochs. I really like Jimmie, and all the others too; but the kissing is simply disgusting."

After a week Teddy kissed his cousins one last time, and he and Alice headed off for the European Continent via London.

Just as they were about to leave London to catch the ferry across the English Channel, Teddy read a newspaper headline that stopped him in his tracks. The headline read, "American President Garfield Shot." Teddy bought the newspaper and read the article, which reported that President Garfield, who had been in office for only four months, had been shot in the arm and back by a man named Charles Guiteau. Guiteau was a disgruntled politician whom Garfield had pushed out of office because of his corrupt ways. The article went on to say that the president was not dead but that the doctors gave him little hope of recovery.

Although Teddy was an ocean away, or perhaps because of it, the assassination attempt bothered him a great deal. He thought back on some of the lines from the letter his father had written to him shortly before he died. "I feel sorry for the country however as it shows the power of partisan politicians who think of nothing higher than their own interests, and I feel for the future. We cannot stand so corrupt a government for any great length of time." Something stirred within Teddy as he thought about his father's words. He wrote in his diary, "Frightful calamity for America.... This means work in the future for all men who wish their country well."

Teddy certainly wished his country well, and he began to think about how he could serve it in a more direct manner. Although he was doing well at law school, he could not imagine himself being a lawyer. Teddy hated the way the law was used to fight against justice rather than for it. Something about going into politics intrigued him, and he decided to investigate more closely what some of his options might be when he got home. But for now he had an adventure in Europe to enjoy.

By the time they got to Switzerland, Teddy felt invigorated. He met some British men at a lodge at the base of the Matterhorn, and when he heard they were going to climb the famous mountain peak, Teddy was envious. Without even consulting Alice, he decided to show them that a Yankee could climb just as well as they could.

Teddy hired two experienced guides, and early the following morning they set out up the mountain. It was a steep, grueling climb, and Teddy was glad when they stopped for the night in a climber's hut carved into the side of the mountain. The floor of the hut was a sheet of solid ice, which made for a cold night.

At four the next morning, they again set out on their assent of the Matterhorn. The guides were eager to get to the summit and back down before the afternoon sun softened the ice and made climbing conditions treacherous. By now the mountain was so steep that even the snow would not stick to its sides, but Teddy kept climbing. Later he remarked that the morning sun greeted them with "a most glorious sunrise which crowned the countless snow peaks and billowy, white clouds with a strange crimson iridescence."

By seven in the morning they had reached the summit. With great satisfaction Teddy took in the view from the top of the Matterhorn. All too soon it was time to start the descent of the mountain, which on such a steep peak proved almost as difficult as climbing it. But by late afternoon Teddy was enjoying a hot bath and a steaming cup of tea in the lodge at the bottom of the mountain. Teddy felt exhilarated by his accomplishment, and his Matterhorn ascent was the highlight of his trip to Europe.

From Switzerland Teddy and Alice traveled down the Rhine and explored Holland and Belgium. Then Alice insisted on a long stay in Paris so that she could have new dresses made for the next season's parties. Teddy was glad to comply.

As the happy couple boarded a steamer for the United States, Teddy thought about what he had experienced on the trip. The wretched, poor conditions in Ireland bothered him, as did the news the week before that President Garfield had finally died from his wounds and Vice President Chester Arthur had been sworn in as president. As never before, Teddy pondered the whole notion of American democracy. He included his conclusions in a letter to one of his friends from Harvard. "This summer I have passed travelling through Europe, and though I have enjoyed it greatly, yet the more I see, the better satisfied I am that I am an American; free born and free bred, where I acknowledge no man as my superior, except for his own worth, or as my inferior, except by his own demerit."

In October 1881, Teddy and Alice celebrated their first wedding anniversary along with Teddy's twenty-third birthday. With Chester Arthur now president, Teddy was happy to be home and able to test the new political climate for himself.

On his first visit back to Morton Hall, Teddy was surprised to find that many of the men gathered there were glad to see him back, especially his Irish friend Joe Murray. Joe explained to Teddy that he had arrived just in time to become the independent candidate for the Twenty-first District's representative in the New York State Assembly at Albany. It was a one-year position, and Joe was sure that Teddy had enough grassroots support to win the nomination.

Teddy knew that there would be obstacles in his way. Rich and refined men such as he did get involved in politics, but not the low-level politics of Manhattan. For a "silk stocking," as men of privilege like Teddy were negatively referred to by many, the only proper way to enter politics was at the top: a good law degree, ten years in practice, and then a run for the United States Senate.

For Teddy, however, ten years was a long time to wait. Besides, he loved to be in the middle of any kind of rough-and-tumble activity, whether it was climbing a mountain or boxing or local politics. Still, entering such a different career was a huge move for someone who really did not need a career at all.

Teddy stalled for a week before allowing Joe to put his name forward as candidate for the district. By then Teddy was sure that Joe was an honest man who would not require special favors for nominating him, and he was also sure that he had his family's backing. Bamie, Conie, and his mother, Mittie, were all enthusiastic about the possibility of Teddy's going into politics. As the three adoring women in his life, they pledged to fold ballots, canvas the neighborhood, and do whatever else they could.

Alice was a little less enthusiastic, since winning the position would involve their moving upstate to

Albany. But Teddy convinced her that this was what he really wanted, so Alice joined the Roosevelt women in supporting her husband.

Once he had made up his mind to run, Teddy threw every ounce of energy he had into winning the seat. He boiled his platform down into one statement: "Strong Republican on state matters, but independent on local and municipal affairs."

Teddy's campaign circular was equally brief.

Dear Sir,

Having been nominated as a candidate for member of Assembly for this District, I would esteem it as a compliment if you honor me with your vote and personal influence on Election Day.

Very Respectfully,
Teddy Roosevelt

When Joe read the letter he smiled. "Ah, Teddy, that may win you support in the brownstones, but you'll have to do a bit more to win the popular vote. Come with me tomorrow night, and I'll start you off doing some proper canvassing."

Joe explained that saloon keepers wielded a lot of grassroots political power in the district. He took Teddy to a saloon on Sixth Avenue, where he introduced him to the keeper. The saloon keeper questioned Teddy about his political beliefs and what he would do for the district if he were elected to the Assembly. Things seemed to be going well until the saloon keeper complained to Teddy about the amount that he had to pay for his liquor license.

"How much is the license fee?" Teddy inquired.

"Two hundred dollars," the saloon keeper replied.

"Two hundred dollars? That's not nearly enough. It ought to be one thousand dollars," Teddy said in his usual forthright manner.

A look of bewilderment spread over the saloon keeper's face, and Joe quickly interrupted the conversation and hustled Teddy outside. He explained that the purpose of canvassing was to garner support for him on Election Day, not to alienate influential saloon keepers and other businessmen. Joe told Teddy that from now on he should stay at his end of town, winning the support of the rich and powerful in the district, while he campaigned for Teddy at the other end of town.

True to his word, Joe campaigned tirelessly while Teddy looked for support among the rich and powerful. The combination worked, and on Election Day, November 9, Teddy won the seat 3,490 votes to 1,989. At twenty-three years of age, Theodore Roosevelt was now an elected politician.

The Assembly convened in Albany on January 2, 1882, and Teddy worked feverishly to get his manuscript on the Naval War of 1812 ready to send to the publisher before he left. He completed it on time while managing to attend many Christmas season social events before setting out for Albany on New Year's Day. Alice had gone to Canada with friends and planned to join him in Albany in a couple of weeks.

Teddy's first days as an assemblyman were telling. He wrote in his journal,

> 3 January. The Legislature has assembled in full force; 128 Assemblymen, containing 61 Republicans in their ranks, and 8 Tammany men among the 67 Democrats. Tammany thus holds the balance of power, and as the split between her [Tammany] and the regular Democrats is very bitter a long deadlock is promised.

Teddy's prediction proved to be correct. The first item of business was for the Assembly to elect a new speaker. Half the votes, sixty-four in all, were required for this process, and the Tammany men, whose group often abused power, refused to vote. Since the Republicans did not have sixty-four members, and the Democrats could field only fifty-nine, the house was deadlocked. Morning after morning Teddy trudged up State Street to answer the roll call in the Assembly chamber, but no business could be conducted until a speaker was chosen. It was obvious to Teddy, even as a first-time assemblyman, that the Tammany men were waiting for one side or the other to cut a deal with them, giving them choice committee positions in return for their votes. Neither side wanted to do this, and Teddy urged the Republicans to outwait the Democrats and "keep their hands clean."

In the meantime Teddy took long walks in the countryside and read everything about the history of New York politics that he could get his hands on. Alice arrived during his second week in Albany, and the two of them set up a small house together.

It took another four weeks, until February 12, before the deadlock was broken and the Democrats made a deal. Once the Assembly was under way, it did not take long before Teddy learned how to be heard. In his high-pitched voice, he would yell, "Mister Spee-kar, Mister Spee-kar." If the speaker refused to acknowledge him, Teddy would march up and down the aisles until he was recognized. Sometimes it took forty minutes, but once he decided he had something to say, Teddy never gave up.

About halfway through the five-month session, Isaac Hunt, one of Teddy's fellow Republicans, told Teddy about a New York State Supreme Court judge named T. R. Westbrooke. According to Isaac, when insurance companies got into financial difficulties, Judge Westbrooke directed them to come under the control of specific receiving companies. The judge's son and cousin were in charge of two of these companies and collected thousands of dollars in unnecessary fees and expenses.

When Teddy investigated this claim of corruption for himself, he found that it was true, and he decided to take his findings to the Assembly. Many of the other assemblymen did not want to hear about corruption, as they were receiving payoffs themselves. But Teddy pushed until the information was allowed to reach the floor of the House.

Nothing this controversial had been talked about in the House for years, and many of the assemblymen closed ranks, protecting their own interests and leaving Teddy on the outside. But this did not bother Teddy as much as a visit from his Uncle James, his father's brother.

Uncle James took Teddy out for lunch, and when they had ordered, he got straight to the point. "You have done well in Albany, so far, lad," he said. "Your father would have been very proud of you, and I know that your mother is."

"Thank you, sir," Teddy replied politely, sensing that this was not the point of the conversation.

"But now it is time for you to leave politics and identify with the right kind of people," Uncle James continued smoothly. "You were a greenhorn when you came here, and you have had your fun. However, I am sure you can see by now that there will always be an inner circle of corporate executives, politicians, lawyers, and judges who control things and obtain the real rewards. If you take them on, it will be at your own peril."

"But if I do not oppose such corruption where I find it, who will, Uncle?" Teddy asked.

Uncle James shook his head. "Some things are too big, even for the Roosevelts, to change, and political corruption is one of those things. Save your energy for something you have a chance of succeeding at."

Teddy sat staring at his tomato soup and roll. Should he heed his uncle's advice? Perhaps it was time to retire to a leisurely life after all. It would certainly be a lot less pressure than confronting corruption in the State Assembly. But if no one took a risk, how would the United States escape the corruption that threatened her future?

Chapter 9

"The Light Has Gone Out of My Life"

Teddy picked up the copy of *Harper's Weekly* and adjusted his glasses. "It is with the greatest satisfaction," he read, "that those who are interested in good government see a young man in the Legislature who, like Mr. Roosevelt, does not know the meaning of fear, and to whom the bluster and bravado of party and political bullies are as absolutely indifferent as the blowing of the wind."

Teddy smiled and made a note to show the article to his mother when he got back to New York City. Although many people had tried to dissuade Teddy from continuing his political career, articles like this made it all seem worthwhile to him. He was making and would continue to make a difference by speaking up, and common people were supporting him.

When the Assembly closed its session that spring, Teddy returned home a wiser and more famous man. Elliot was waiting for him when he got home. He had just returned from his world trip. Teddy was looking forward to spending the summer with his brother, but his excitement soon turned to frustration. Elliot, it appeared, had spent much of his trip drinking heavily, and he continued the habit back in New York. Everyone noticed it. Teddy talked to him about his problem, but Elliot insisted that he was just having a good time and would settle down to a regular life soon enough.

Teddy was glad to get away to Oyster Bay with Alice for the summer and leave Elliot in New York to attend the usual round of parties. Now that he was a well-traveled young bachelor with a host of funny stories to tell, Elliot was even more popular with the ladies.

Meanwhile Conie was preparing for her marriage to Douglas Robinson, a Scottish-American millionaire. The ceremony took place in August, and it was a lavish affair. Teddy was a little embarrassed about all the attention he received at the wedding. He had just been voted in for a second term in the legislature, and everyone wanted to congratulate him on winning the election.

Teddy's second year in Albany started off well. He won the Republican nomination to be speaker of the house but was beaten by the Democrats' candidate. At twenty-four Teddy found himself the leader of the opposition, and he tried his best to do the job well. Sometimes he made mistakes, mainly because he was unwilling to compromise and work with other members of the Assembly. But over time he began to realize that he could retain his integrity and make some compromises at the same time.

The five-month term passed quickly, and at the end of it, Alice had some wonderful news—she was expecting a baby on Valentine's Day, 1884. Teddy was overcome with excitement. Conie had just delivered her first child, a son named Theodore, and Teddy could imagine the two children growing up together, especially since he had bought the house next to Corinne and Douglas on 45th Street for him and Alice to live in.

Teddy had also bought ninety-five acres of land at Oyster Bay, where he planned to build a grand summerhouse overlooking the bay. He intended to call the place Leeholm after Alice's family. And now that Alice was pregnant, he decided it was time to start building the house. He instructed architects to begin drawing up plans for the place. The house was to be spacious, with ten bedrooms, a large library, huge fireplaces, and a wraparound porch where he and Alice could sit and watch their children play.

The excitement of becoming a father made Teddy more restless than ever, and he decided to do something to release his energy. When a retired naval officer named Commander H. H. Gorringe invited Teddy to accompany him on a hunting trip to the Dakota Territory, Teddy eagerly agreed. He dreamed about the antelope, deer, and buffalo he could hunt there.

A week before the two men were due to leave, Commander Gorringe had to pull out of the trip, but Teddy was so excited about the trip that he decided to go alone. On September 3 he caught a train from New York to Chicago, where he transferred to another train, which carried him into Dakota Territory. This was farther west than he had ever been, and the scenery thrilled him, especially the kaleidoscope of colors the setting sun unleashed across the land.

At three in the morning, the train stopped amid the sagebrush and let Teddy off at the tiny town of Little Missouri, in the Badlands. When the sun came up, Teddy set about hiring a guide to take him hunting. This proved to be more difficult than he thought it would be. Most of the residents of Little Missouri were reluctant to take an inexperienced easterner, or tenderfoot, as they called him, out into the wilderness, especially one wearing thick glasses. Finally Teddy managed to hire a Canadian named Joe Ferris, and the two of them set out.

At the end of eight days, Teddy had had close encounters with rattlesnakes, shot two stags, had his horse sink in quicksand, ridden through torrential rain, and endured biting cold mornings, but he had not yet seen or shot a buffalo. On the ninth day his luck changed. As Teddy was riding along through countryside bisected by narrow, deep ravines, he came upon fresh buffalo tracks. He dismounted and followed the tracks on foot. A short while later the tracks led him to the edge of a ravine. As he peered over the edge, there at the bottom was a large buffalo bull feeding. Stealthily Teddy crept up on the beast until he was within range to get a good shot at the buffalo. He raised his gun and squeezed the trigger. The bullet hit the bull at the back of its shoulder. The bull began to run, but it dropped dead within a hundred yards. Teddy was ecstatic; he finally had his buffalo. The animal's head and the antlers from the stags were sent back to New York to be mounted and ready to be hung on the walls of the new summerhouse as soon as it was finished.

Teddy returned to New York very pleased with the trip. Not only had he shot a buffalo, but also he had bought a herd of cattle, which Joe Ferris's brother Sylvane would manage and feed on the open range of Dakota Territory. The future looked bright as Teddy contemplated working in Albany during the late winter and spring, staying at Leeholm in the summer, and riding the open range in Dakota Territory in the fall. Teddy chuckled to himself as he thought of a son, or several sons, following their father through the Badlands on horseback. Teddy assured himself that the future was coming into delightful focus.

That December Elliot married Anna Hall in a wedding that was dubbed the social event of the year. Anna was the oldest daughter of a wealthy family, and the Roosevelts hoped that marriage would tame Elliot. Teddy rented his house on 45th Street to the newlyweds and moved with Alice back into his mother's house. Alice was only two months away from giving birth, and Teddy felt it would be better for her to be living under his mother's watchful eye during this time.

On January 2, 1884, Teddy set out for Albany to begin his third term as an assemblyman. He was quickly named the chairman of the Cities Committee, and his main aim was to weaken the corrupt influence of the Tammany men. To do this, Teddy ordered that committee hearings be held every Friday, Saturday, and Monday in New York City. Any citizen who had a grievance could come before the committee and state his or her problem.

All sorts of injustices were uncovered as news spread that Assemblyman Roosevelt would listen to and investigate the claims of even the lowest members of society. It came to light that the sheriff's office and the Ludlow Street jail were hotbeds of extortion. The inmates at the jail lived under dripping sewage pipes and had to eat out of toilet buckets unless they could come up with $250 to "buy" a better cell. It was in this kind of forum that Teddy realized that he had found his voice at last. Like his father before him, he cared about the needs of the poor and destitute, and he was now in a position to do something about those needs.

Being on the committee also meant that Teddy could spend more time with Alice as she neared the end of her pregnancy. On Monday, February 11, Teddy took the train from New York back to Albany. He hated to leave Alice, but he knew she was in good hands. Conie and baby Theodore were staying at the house, and Bamie was there as well. Teddy's mother, Mittie, was there too, but she had a slight cold and was concerned about giving it to Alice.

That evening, as Teddy settled into his boardinghouse room, a hand-carried letter arrived from Alice. He read it quickly:

> Darling Thee,
>
> I hated so to leave you this afternoon. I don't think you need feel worried about my being sick as the Dr told me this afternoon that I would not need my nurse before Thursday—I am feeling well tonight but am very much worried over your mother, her fever is still very high and the Dr is rather afraid of typhoid, it is not the least catching. I will write again to-morrow and let you know just how she is—don't say any thing about it till then. I do love my dear Thee so much, I wish I could have my little new baby soon.
>
> Ever Your loving wife,
> Alice

Typhoid! The thought alarmed Teddy, but as he read Alice's letter again, he calmed down. Alice knew how to reach him, and if his mother got worse he would know about it as soon as possible. In the meantime he had to prepare to report on fourteen bills that the Cities Committee was recommending to cut corruption in New York City.

Late the next night Teddy received a telegram. It was wonderful news. Alice had delivered an eight-and-three-quarter-pound girl, and all was well. On the way to the Assembly the next morning, Teddy stopped to buy cigars to hand out. He wanted everyone to share with him the joy of his daughter's birth.

That day, February 13, dragged on, and Teddy's thoughts were often with his wife and their new baby, whom they had agreed upon ahead of time to name Alice. About three o'clock in the afternoon another telegram arrived for Teddy. He opened it and read, "Come home immediately. Both patients much worse. Bamie."

Both patients? Teddy stared blankly at the piece of paper. Both patients—was that his mother and his wife, or his wife and the baby? He couldn't tell, but he hastily excused himself from the room and ran to the train station.

It was a particularly cold day, and fog clung to the banks of the Hudson River. Some of the trains had been canceled because of the lack of visibility, but Teddy managed to catch one bound for New York City. Once aboard he settled himself for the ride. There was no point in looking out the window; everything was shrouded in gray, yet Teddy stared anyway. He thought of the time six years ago when he had rushed home to his father, only to find he had died. He wondered if he was about to repeat that awful experience.

The train blasted its horn continuously and crept through the fog toward New York. It arrived at Grand Central Station at midnight, several hours behind schedule. As soon as it had pulled to a halt at the platform, Teddy leapt off and headed down East 42nd Street. The city was eerily silent as he groped his way along. The streetlights were small pools of yellow against the fog, giving off no real light to help him keep his bearings.

Eventually, Teddy made it to the house on 57th Street. A light was burning in Alice's third-floor window, and he took that as a good sign. Then Elliot emerged from the doorway. His hair was disheveled, and he looked dazed. Teddy pushed past him and ran up the stairs two at a time. He rushed into Alice's room and knelt beside her bed. Taking her in his arms he said, "My poor darling, I am sorry I took so long to get here."

Alice looked right past him. Her china blue eyes were vacant.

Teddy started to sob. "My poor darling, what is wrong with you? Don't you know me?"

He felt a presence behind him and turned his head to see Bamie standing there. "The doctor says it's Bright's disease. Alice's kidneys have failed with the strain of the pregnancy. Oh, Teddy, I am so sorry. There is nothing we can do," she said, beginning to sob herself.

Teddy stayed on his knees for a long time, holding Alice and hoping against hope that she would recover.

Sometime in the early hours of the morning Elliot walked into the room. "You'd better come and see Mother, Teddy. I didn't tell you before because one grief at a time is enough for any man to bear, but Mother does have typhoid fever. If you want to say good-bye to her, you had better come now."

Appalled by the words he had just heard, Teddy rose from his knees and followed his brother down to the second floor. His mother lay in her bed with Bamie and Conie standing on one side of it. Mittie Roosevelt was breathing in short, sharp breaths when Teddy bent down to kiss her. Like Alice, she did not seem to recognize him.

Minutes later her breath became shallow and then finally stopped. The clock struck 3 A.M. Teddy wanted to sink down into a chair and weep, but his mind was on Alice.

Wearily, Teddy climbed the stairs again and took up his vigil beside Alice. Various maids offered him coffee and food, but he would not take them. Conie came in with baby Alice in her arms, but Teddy could hardly look at his new daughter. His only concern was for his wife.

At two o'clock in the afternoon, Alice Roosevelt died. Numbly, and with tears in his eyes, Teddy Roosevelt drew a big, black cross in his diary and wrote, "The light has gone out of my life."

News quickly spread of the double tragedy that had befallen Teddy, losing his mother and wife on the same day in the same house. Flowers and condolences flowed into the house, but they meant little to Teddy. He was too dazed to notice them.

Chapter 10

In the Badlands

The Fifth Avenue Presbyterian Church was filled to overflowing with two thousand mourners. Teddy sat in the front row with Conie, Bamie, Elliot, and Alice's father. Two rosewood caskets lay side by side at the altar, each covered in roses and lily-of-the-valley sprigs. Dr. Hall, the minister, stood up and recited an opening prayer. Following this the choir sang "Rock of Ages," and then the sermon began. Teddy tried to concentrate on what Dr. Hall was saying, but it was impossible. Every time he looked at the two coffins, one bearing his twenty-two-year-old wife and the other his forty-eight-year-old mother, tears blurred his eyes.

Teddy was not the only person in the church finding it hard to control his emotions; sobbing and nose blowing punctuated the entire service.

Toward the end, when the minister prayed that God would take care of baby Alice, he, too, began to weep. It was the most awful experience of Teddy's life, and by the time the family returned from the cemetery, Teddy was totally exhausted. He locked himself in his room and wept.

The following morning baby Alice was baptized in the same church. Teddy's Aunt Anna had cut a lock of Alice's hair and put it in a locket around the infant's neck. Teddy held the child during the service, but as soon as it was over, he gave her to Bamie. "Here, take baby Lee," he said, unable to even pronounce his dead wife's first name and using her family name instead. "Raise her as your own. Tell me how much you spend on her each month, and I will repay you."

Bamie took the little girl and cuddled her. "Are you sure, Teddy?" she asked.

Teddy nodded. "How can I raise a baby? She'll be much better off with you than me," he said.

Bamie didn't say any more as she carried the baby out of the church. Later that week Bamie took on the first of many other responsibilities. Teddy wanted to finish Leeholm, the summerhouse at Oyster Bay, but he could not bear to think of the happy times that he and Alice had spent poring over the plans. So he asked Bamie to supervise the project until it was finished.

There did not seem any need for the large house on 57th Street either, and plans were made to sell it. A buyer was found almost immediately, and once again it fell to Bamie to clear everything out and divide it among the Roosevelt siblings. As Teddy watched the furniture being carried away, he felt like his whole life had been dismantled and parceled off.

Within two weeks of Alice's death, Teddy was back in Albany. He wanted to bury himself in work and never speak of his dead wife again. Instead he would keep Alice locked away—young, pretty, and vibrant—in his memory until the day he died.

The Assembly kept his mind occupied until May, but he could not imagine going back to New York City after that. New York held too many memories for him. Instead he decided his time in politics was over and he would go to the Badlands in Dakota Territory and live quietly there, out of the public eye.

Once again Teddy traveled west by train. When he arrived, he bought himself a horse and began wandering through the barren landscape strewn with bones and buffalo skulls. These and the strange-shaped buttes suited Teddy's mood, and mile after mile he thought about his life. As he rode, his heart and mind slowly began to heal, and he headed toward the Maltese Cross Ranch, where he set up headquarters for his stay in the Badlands.

The herd of cattle Teddy had bought the summer before now lived on the ranch, and he was glad to see they were prospering. Teddy used the money he had inherited from his mother's estate to double the size of the herd and embraced the life of a rancher. Sometimes he rode for twelve hours a day, rounding up cattle, checking on a small herd of buffalo on the property, and hunting bears.

When summer arrived, Teddy headed back to New York. He stayed with Bamie and baby Alice Lee on Madison Avenue for several days and visited Elliot and Anna and their baby daughter, Eleanor, and Conie and Douglas and little Theodore. He was delighted to see Eleanor and Theodore, but he found it difficult to spend time with Alice Lee. She had a pert, turned-up nose and blonde ringlets and was clearly her mother's daughter.

After his stop in the city, Teddy moved on to Leeholm, his now-finished summerhouse at Oyster Bay where he had imagined raising a tribe of children with Alice.

While staying at Leeholm, Teddy slowly began to reenter high society. He started to dance again and ran into his childhood friend Edith Carow. Soon the two of them were inseparable. Edith had known the Roosevelts all her life, and Teddy found it easy to talk with her about his mother's death, though he never talked to anyone about Alice's death, since it was too private and painful for him.

In the fall Teddy headed back to the Badlands to resume his life on the range. From time to time he boarded a train and headed back east to New York to visit his family. In the summer of 1885, he once again went to stay at Leeholm, in Oyster Bay, where he and Edith spent a lot of time together. By November 1885 Teddy realized that he still wanted a wife and family, and his thoughts turned to Edith. He knew the timing was not good; it was only a year and a half since Alice had died. He and Edith agreed to keep their engagement a secret for at least a year. They both hoped the year would pass quickly.

After they became engaged, Teddy headed back to the Badlands, and Edith went to England with her mother and sister Emily. It was not a pleasure trip for Edith but a necessity. Her father had squandered the family's wealth on drinking and gambling and then died of alcohol poisoning. Little money was left in his estate, so the three Carow women decided to set out for Europe, where the cost of living was much cheaper than in New York.

Back in Dakota Territory, Teddy was content once again. He knew many changes were in store for him, so he tried to enjoy each day. He wrote two books, *Hunting Trips of a Ranchman* and *Ranch Life and the Hunting Trail.* As it turned out, however, his most exciting adventure had nothing to do with hunting at all but with a missing boat.

It was early spring 1886 when Teddy discovered that the boat used to ferry supplies across the Little Missouri River to the ranch had been stolen. He immediately suspected Mike Finnegan, who lived nearby with two other men named Burnsted and Pfaffenbach. The three men were known horse thieves in the area, and Teddy decided that they had stolen the boat to flee down the river ahead of a posse intent on capturing and hanging them.

Although the boat was worth only about thirty dollars, Teddy decided that the principle of justice needed to be enforced, even in this remote corner of the prairie. So while two ranch hands busied themselves building a new boat, Teddy made plans to chase the thieves downriver.

As soon as the vessel was ready, Teddy and the two ranch hands climbed aboard. Along with his rifle and a supply of food, Teddy took with him a camera and several books to read. An icy wind howled, and ice floes on the river buffeted the boat, threatening to sink it on several occasions. The men traveled downstream for three days. They were about a hundred miles from the ranch when Teddy spotted the stolen boat. Nearby he saw smoke curling up from a campfire. The men pulled their boat ashore a little upstream and crept up on the campsite. Only Pfaffenbach was in camp, and he was taken totally by surprise. He explained that the other two men were out hunting and would be back soon.

Teddy and his two companions lay in wait for them. As soon as the two men arrived back in camp, Teddy and his companions cocked and aimed their rifles and ordered the two outlaws to throw down their weapons. Burnsted immediately did as he was told; Teddy noticed his knees were shaking. But Mike Finnegan held on to his rifle, his eyes darting around the camp looking for an avenue of escape. When he did not drop his gun, Teddy stepped forward until he was just several feet from Finnegan. He aimed his rifle squarely at Finnegan's chest and once again ordered him to drop his weapon. This time the thief complied, cursing Teddy as he laid down his rifle.

Because of the wintry weather conditions, Teddy decided that it would be hopeless to go back upriver and that they ought to head downstream with the prisoners to Mandan, about 150 miles away, the nearest sizeable town. They began poling their way downstream, but the going was slow. Conditions on the river were terrible. In places the river was almost completely iced over, greatly impeding their progress. In other places large chunks of ice smashed against the boat, and in its overloaded state Teddy wondered whether it might not fly apart from the stress.

At the end of six days, the men had eaten all their food and there was no game around to kill and eat, and so the prisoners and their captors ended up eating flour mixed with muddy river water.

When they came to a cowboy camp at the side of the river, Teddy decided on a change of plan. Instead of taking the prisoners farther downstream, he would take them overland to Dickinson, about a day and a half's travel away, where they could be turned over to the local sheriff. Meanwhile his two companions would take the boat on down to Mandan and return it upstream to the ranch when the ice in the river cleared.

Teddy hired a wagon and team of horses from a nearby rancher, who was surprised he hadn't just hung the prisoners when he caught them, and set out for Dickinson. Although ice still clogged the river, on land the spring thaw had set in, and Teddy soon found himself sloshing through knee-deep mud. The men spent that night in a small, run-down hut. Teddy did not sleep; he sat with his back against the door and his gun at the ready lest his prisoners try to make a break. At dawn the men set out again trudging through the mud. Thirty-six hours after setting out from the river, they came to Dickinson. Teddy, covered in mud from head to toe and his feet badly blistered, happily turned his prisoners over to the local sheriff.

A trial soon followed, and Finnegan and Burnsted were sentenced to three years in the territorial penitentiary in Bismarck. In the end Teddy decided not to press charges against Pfaffenbach, saying, "He did not have enough sense to do anything good or bad." After the trial the old German came up and thanked Teddy incessantly for not pressing charges against him. Teddy laughed; it was the first time anyone had ever thanked him for calling him a fool!

By the time Teddy's blisters had fully healed, summer was almost over and it was time for him to leave the Badlands. Little rain had fallen that summer, and most of the cattle had to be sent to market because there was not enough grass for them to eat. Teddy resisted the urge to sell off all of his stock, hoping that better days were ahead for the growing cattle industry. Leaving the remains of his herd in good hands, Teddy returned to New York City ready to find his place in the world again.

Teddy had scarcely unpacked his bags and settled into Bamie's house when a group of influential Republicans came to call on him. They wanted to nominate him as the party's candidate for mayor of New York. Teddy had followed the situation from a distance, but he knew that the Republicans had very little chance of winning the election. Still, the Republicans had to field a candidate, and they hoped to run a tough campaign, which they thought Teddy could energize.

Teddy accepted the nomination, and he was immediately dubbed the Cowboy Candidate. He worked eighteen hours a day for the next three weeks, attending rallies, talking to reporters, and visiting factories and worksites.

Even in the midst of the campaign, Teddy was a realist. He quietly booked passage for two aboard the *Etruria* under the names of Mr. and Miss Merrifield. The ship was due to depart New York for England four days after the election.

Teddy did lose the election, by a huge margin, and was relieved to soon be on his way to England to marry Edith Carow. His sister Bamie accompanied him on the trip. It did not take long for the other passengers to work out that Teddy Roosevelt was on board, and soon Teddy had more dinner appointments than he could handle. He also met a young British diplomat named Cecil Spring Rice. "Springy," as he was nicknamed, and Teddy became good friends. By the time the voyage was over, Teddy had asked him to be best man at his wedding.

A whirlwind of activity took place once Teddy arrived in England. The wedding took place at St. George's Church, Hanover Square, London, on December 2, 1886. For their honeymoon the new Mr. and Mrs. Roosevelt toured Europe.

While the couple were in Florence, Teddy read about the worst blizzards to hit the Badlands in living memory. According to the newspapers, all of the livestock in the region, along with many of the frontier families, had frozen to death. Teddy was shocked by the news, which meant that his large investment in the herd of cattle was gone. This would be a significant financial setback, as he had invested a great deal of his money in the herd, money he could have lived on and collected interest on if it hadn't been lost.

His inheritance diminished, Teddy broke the news to Edith that they would have to economize, perhaps even sell the Leeholm house in Oyster Bay. Edith was horrified at the idea of losing the summerhouse and promised to do whatever she could to cut costs. The financial crunch was made doubly hard by the knowledge that Teddy would soon have another mouth to feed, as Edith had just learned that she was pregnant. Teddy and Edith returned to New York City in March, unsure of what the future held for them.

Chapter 11

Civil Service Commissioner

The summer of 1887 passed quietly, with few visitors to the Roosevelts' house at Oyster Bay. Teddy had renamed Leeholm so that Edith would feel more at home there. It was now called Sagamore Hill. Teddy filled his days playing polo and writing a book on Gouverneur Morris, a Revolutionary-era politician and diplomat. Midway through the summer, Bamie came to visit and brought Alice Lee with her. When Bamie left, three-year-old Alice Lee stayed on. Edith insisted that she live with them now and that she raise Alice as if she were her own daughter.

As the birth of the new baby drew near, Teddy became very anxious over Edith's health. Thankfully, everything went well, and on September 13, 1887, Edith delivered a large and very healthy baby boy. They named him Theodore Jr., and everyone was thrilled except for Alice Lee, who complained that little Ted was "a howling Polly parrot."

With his wife doing so well, Teddy decided to take a hunting trip. He was gone for a month, a month that opened his eyes to a developing problem. The wildlife in the Badlands was disappearing—fast. The buffalo, elk, and grizzly bears were gone, and many of Teddy's favorite birds did not return to their summer homes. Most startling of all was the effect that years of beaver trapping had produced. The beavers were all gone, which meant that there were no new beaver dams. As the old dams rotted away, ponds emptied out, leaving nowhere for the fish and wildfowl to live. Plant life was suffering as well. Even the wild-plum bushes had been poisoned off by cow dung.

For the first time in his life Teddy saw how the death of one animal or plant species affected all the other species around it. The Badlands was no longer the teeming natural paradise it had once been but was now a forlorn and decaying landscape. Something stirred within Teddy. He decided he had to do what he could to save America's wildlife and habitat for future generations.

Back in New York Teddy invited a dozen of his wealthiest friends to dinner at Bamie's house. As they ate, Teddy described to the guests what he had seen and how the killing of one species sent other species into rapid decline. Using all of his persuasive skills, Teddy convinced the men to form a club. The aim of the club was to study and record observations about the natural history of wild animals and to work for the preservation of forest regions as nurseries and reservations for woodland creatures that would otherwise die as the West was settled.

The men called themselves the Boone & Crockett Club, after two of Teddy's heroes, Daniel Boone and Davy Crockett. The club was the first conservation club in the United States and in the whole world, as far as Teddy could tell. Teddy recruited lawyers, politicians, and leading scientists into its ranks.

The establishing of the club gave Teddy another idea. He would write a book on the western expansion of the United States, starting in 1774, when Daniel Boone first crossed the Allegheny Mountains, and covering up until 1836, when Davy Crockett was killed at the Alamo. The name of the book was to be *The Winning of the West.*

Teddy had a wonderful time researching the book. He traveled to Kentucky, Tennessee, and Washington, D.C., unearthing old documents and collecting unpublished diaries from the period. Putnam Publishers wrote him a contract for the book, which was to be spread over two volumes and was to be completed in a year and a half. However, when he sat down to write the book in April 1888, Teddy found the task daunting. He had so much material to work into the manuscript, and he wanted to do a thorough job.

When Benjamin Harrison asked Teddy in 1888 to help him with his campaign for president, Teddy gladly welcomed the distraction from his writing. He set off on a speaking tour of Minnesota, Michigan, and Illinois and loved every minute of it. He was delighted when Harrison won the election and the Republicans took the Senate and the House of Representatives.

With the change from a Democratic to a Republican administration in the White House, many Democrats lost their government jobs. Their replacements were people the new president wanted in his administration, and one of these people was Teddy Roosevelt.

On April 27, 1889, just after Teddy had completed the second volume of *The Winning of the West,* Henry Cabot Lodge came to Sagamore Hill to visit Teddy. He brought news from Washington, D.C., that President Harrison wanted to appoint Teddy as a U.S. Civil Service commissioner. The salary of $3,500 a year was low, but Teddy took the job anyway. While writing and researching *The Winning of the West,* he had realized that his heart lay in politics after all.

A month later Teddy sat at his desk in Washington, D.C. At age thirty he was youngest of the three commissioners, but he was their natural leader. The Civil Service Commission had been established in 1883 to administer the Pendleton Act, which required open competitive examinations in filling some government jobs. The Pendleton Act had been passed in an attempt to undercut the so-called spoils system, whereby friends and political supporters of the ruling party were given plum government jobs in return for their support. This meant that many ineffectual people were promoted to important civil-service positions ahead of better-qualified and more able men.

With his education, experience, and disdain for corruption, Teddy Roosevelt was qualified for the job. But not everyone in the new administration was excited about his being made a Civil Service commissioner. Despite the Pendleton Act, the spoils system had not gone away, and the last thing many people in Washington wanted was an activist in the Civil Service Commission who would attempt to enforce the letter of the law. And that is what Teddy intended to do. From his experience as an assemblyman in New York, he knew that fighting corruption in the civil service was an important issue in restoring the confidence of the people in their government. Teddy declared, "No republic can permanently endure when its politics are corrupt and base. The spoils system, the application in politics of the degrading doctrine that to the victors belong the spoils, produces corruption and degradation.... The spoils-monger and the spoils-seeker invariably breed the bribe-taker and the bribe-giver, the embezzler of public funds, and the corrupter of voters."

The great irony that presented itself to Teddy when he arrived in Washington was that many jobs in the U.S. Civil Service Commission, including his, had been parceled out as part of the spoils system. Civil Service commissioners had a reputation for being lazy and ineffectual at enforcing the law. They were much more at home enjoying leisurely lunches at a nearby oyster house on Louisiana Avenue than being in their offices seeing that the Pendleton Act was uniformly applied. Teddy realized that he would have to reform the very organization he oversaw before it could effectively oversee other federal agencies.

Teddy threw himself into the task. He set a pace of work that was shocking to his fellow workers as he set about overhauling the examinations that workers had to take for entry into and advancement in the civil service. "Plain, commonsense questions" ought to be asked in the exams, he declared. Teddy also believed that, in making civil-service appointments, practical experience ought to be emphasized more than just theoretical knowledge. It made no sense to him that passing a spelling test was more important in considering whether a person should be appointed a border patrolman in the western states than whether the man could shoot straight, ride a horse well, and read cattle brands at a glance. Such practical skills were far more important than passing a spelling test if the person was to do his job well.

While he was busy reforming the way the Civil Service Commission performed its function, Teddy began to reach out and apply the Pendleton Act uniformly. He traveled to New York City to investigate charges of corruption in the customhouse there. His investigation revealed that a number of questions on a recent civil-service exam had been leaked to candidates ahead of the test for fifty dollars. He issued a scathing report on the affair, calling for the immediate dismissal of three officials in the customhouse and the prosecution of one of them. Newspapers jumped on the story, cheering on those who wanted to see reform in the civil service and sending chills down the spine of those in Washington who still supported the spoils system.

When Teddy next heard what had gone on in the post office, he was very angry. In the six weeks between Benjamin Harrison's being sworn in as president and Teddy's being appointed a Civil Service commissioner, thirty thousand fourth-class postmasters had been removed from their jobs and replaced by Republicans. The man responsible for this was John Wanamaker, the new postmaster general. Wanamaker was himself a product of the spoils system. He was a wealthy retailer from Philadelphia who had served as President Harrison's campaign finance chairman and had been "rewarded" for his efforts with the plum job of postmaster general.

When Teddy heard of breaches of the civil-service law in the Indianapolis post office, he thought it a great opportunity to do something to rectify what had gone on in the postal service after the election. He and his two fellow Civil Service commissioners, Charles Lyman, a fellow Republican, and Hugh Thompson, a Democrat, set out for the Midwest to investigate. The fact that Indianapolis was the hometown of Benjamin Harrison and that the postmaster there, William Wallace, was a good friend of the president, helped to bring the public's attention to such corruption.

After an investigation, Teddy forced Wallace to fire three crooked employees of the post office. One of them was reputed to be a professional gambler, and all three, who had been fired by the previous Democratic postmaster, had been rehired under the new Republican administration. In addition, Wallace promised to scrupulously observe and enforce the civil-service law in the future.

From Indianapolis Teddy and the other two commissioners moved on to Milwaukee, where there were reports of widespread corruption. Upon arriving in Milwaukee, Teddy declared George Paul, the postmaster there, to be "about as thorough-faced a scoundrel as I ever saw." It turned out that Paul was forcing Hamilton Shidy, a post office superintendent, to alter downward the examination marks of more qualified applicants to make it look as if the men Paul had given jobs to were the most qualified. On at least one occasion, Paul had watched as Shidy altered the marks. Shidy handed Teddy a wad of illegal orders, written in Paul's handwriting, instructing him to do this. However, Shidy did not tell Teddy this before securing from him a promise of protection in return for his testimony. Teddy readily agreed, though it was a decision that would cause him much anguish in the future.

Back in Washington the three commissioners prepared a report on the situation in Milwaukee. In it they noted that "[George Paul] had grossly and habitually violated the law, and had done it in a peculiarly revolting and underhanded manner.

His conduct merits the severest punishment...and we recommend his immediate removal." When they had completed their report, they submitted it to the president.

Again Teddy's actions delighted those clamoring for reform of the civil service and stuck in the craw of those who still believed in the spoils system, and none more so than John Wanamaker, who began scheming of ways to get back at Teddy.

All this action kept Teddy in the sweltering heat of Washington for most of the summer instead of at Oyster Bay, where he longed to be. Edith, who was now pregnant with their second child, was staying there with the children, and the family would join him in Washington after the baby was born.

Teddy waited to see what action the White House would take regarding the situation in the Milwaukee post office. But before the president had done anything, George Paul retaliated. He dismissed Hamilton Shidy from his job for treachery and insubordination. Teddy had promised to protect the man in return for his testimony, and he angrily stormed off to see Wanamaker and complain about the situation to him. But the postmaster general refused to intervene.

Shidy's firing put Teddy in a difficult situation. Teddy had made a promise to the man, yet Shidy was also a self-confessed falsifier of government documents. Teddy wrestled with what to do, and eventually he persuaded the superintendent of the census bureau to quietly find a job for Shidy in the bureau. Once again Teddy went to talk to

Wanamaker, who agreed to the transfer of Shidy from the post office to the census bureau.

Finally, on August 5, 1889, Teddy was summoned to the White House, where President Harrison informed him that rather than dismiss George Paul outright, he had decided to accept Paul's letter of resignation. This was a bitter blow to Teddy, who felt that the president had squandered a golden opportunity to make a stand on corruption in the civil service and had chosen to let Paul off easily.

As he so often did in times of frustration, Teddy headed west for a break, this time to the foothills of the Rocky Mountains in Montana. It was a trip that would nearly cost him his life. One night he made camp in a clearing beside a stream in a valley. As dusk descended over the valley, he decided to go and see if he could shoot a grouse for dinner. He climbed to the crest of a ridge and looked over into the next valley. He spotted a grizzly bear below, rumbling along. Teddy had a perfect shot at the beast, so he raised his rifle and fired. The bullet hit the bear in the side. The bear let out a roar and raced into a thicket of laurel. Teddy followed. He could hear the bear moaning in the bushes, but he did not want to follow it into the thicket for fear that it might still be strong enough to attack him.

Teddy's instincts were right. Moments later the bushes parted and the bear lunged out. It turned its head to look at Teddy, frothy blood dripping from its mouth. Instantaneously Teddy fired his rifle again, this time hitting the bear in the shoulder.

Still the great beast would not go down. It let out another roar and charged at Teddy, who again fired his rifle. This time the bullet went through the bear's chest, but still the bear did not stop. Teddy's heart pounded in his chest. The grizzly was now just feet away. As the bear lunged at him with its mouth wide open and its menacing teeth laid bare, Teddy fired for the fourth time. The bullet entered the bear's mouth. As he fired, Teddy dived to the side, narrowly missing coming into contact with the beast's outstretched paw. The bear's momentum carried it forward, and the animal fell to the ground, violently convulsing and then rolling over on its back, dead.

Teddy was relieved to see the grizzly finally dead, and slowly his own heart rate returned to normal. He skinned the animal and cut off its head, which, along with the bearskin, was sent back to Oyster Bay to adorn the floor of Sagamore Hill.

Following his trip west, Teddy returned to Washington refreshed and glad to be alive. Again he threw himself tirelessly into enforcing the civil-service law.

Teddy was working in his office in Washington on October 10 when a telegram arrived for him from Oyster Bay. Edith had given birth prematurely to a second son, whom they had agreed they would name Kermit if the child was a boy. Teddy left immediately for Oyster Bay. When he finally arrived at Sagamore Hill at four in the morning, after a frustrating train delay, he was relieved to find his wife and son both doing well.

For the next two weeks, Teddy stayed at the summerhouse nursing his wife back to full strength. And now that Edith had given birth, it was time for the family to move to Washington, D.C.

Washington was a beautiful city in which to live and work. It had wide, tree-lined avenues, abundant parks and squares, and magnificent architecture. But it was also a very expensive city in which to live. Teddy finally found a house he could afford to rent at 1820 Jefferson Place off Connecticut Avenue. The place was only a tenth the size of Sagamore Hill, and it cost $2,400 a year to rent. It would cost $1,000 a year for food and another $300 for gas and coal to heat and light the house. As the family moved in, Teddy wondered how he was going to pay for it all on his commissioner's salary of $3,500. Once again he thought about selling Sagamore Hill, and once again Edith begged him not to, promising to economize and do her best with the limited budget.

Another challenge awaited Teddy upon his return to Washington. News had gotten out that Teddy used his influence to get a new job for Hamilton Shidy, and those opposed to civil-service reform were calling for a congressional investigation in hopes of embarrassing Teddy and forcing his resignation.

Finally, on January 27, 1890, Congress ordered an investigation into what was now being dubbed the Roosevelt/Shidy affair. Representative Hamilton G. Ewart of South Carolina was chosen to head the investigation. Ewart was a staunch supporter of the spoils system, and in the days of hearings that followed, Teddy noticed that Ewart seemed to relish attacking him at every turn. Teddy mounted an all-out defense, contending that he had done nothing wrong and that John Wanamaker knew of and approved the transfer of Shidy to the census bureau. Wanamaker was called to testify. He was visibly angry about having to do so, but under intense questioning from Teddy, he finally admitted through clenched teeth that he had indeed known of and approved the transfer.

It was not until June 1890 that the report on the investigation was released. Teddy breathed a sigh of relief when he read it. He would not have to resign his post as commissioner after all. The document declared that "the public service had been greatly benefitted, and the law, on the whole, well-executed" by all three of the Civil Service commissioners. "We find that Commissioners Roosevelt and Thompson have discharged their duties with entire fidelity and integrity." The report did single out Commissioner Lyman for some criticism on another matter, though.

Relieved to be exonerated, Teddy raced home to give Edith the good news.

Several days after the release of the report, Teddy went to visit Henry Adams at his home on Lafayette Square across from the White House. Adams's grandfather, John Quincy Adams, and his great grandfather, John Adams, had both served as president. Henry and Teddy had become friends during Teddy's time in Washington, and the two would often meet in the evenings to talk. As he passed the White House this particular evening, Teddy stopped to admire the place. His heart beat faster as he recalled the words of Fräulein Anna to his mother in Dresden, Germany, many years before. "Who knows, he may become even president of the United States," she had said. The thought struck Teddy, *Possibly—possibly—I might indeed one day occupy this place as president.*

Chapter 12

Assistant Secretary of the Navy

In September 1890, Teddy, Edith, Bamie, Conie, and her husband, Douglas, headed west together on a trip. First they stopped in the Badlands, where Teddy showed them the sights of his many adventures. From there they headed farther west to Yellowstone National Park, where they traveled on horseback throughout the park. They climbed to the Continental Divide and marveled at the thundering waterfalls and explosive geysers dotting the landscape. Edith in particular enjoyed the experience, and Teddy noted in a letter to his mother-in-law, "I have rarely seen Edith enjoy anything more than she did...[on]...the trip through the Yellowstone Park."

Teddy enjoyed the trek through the park as well, but he was perplexed by the conditions he found there. The Yellowstone country had been set aside as a national park in 1872, but now, eighteen years later, the pristine landscape was being recklessly exploited. The law that created the park had failed to include any enforcement provisions to keep the park in its natural state. As a result, the buffalo, elk, and other animals that roamed in the park were being hunted mercilessly. At the same time, various entrepreneurial businessmen were busy building resorts with no concern as to how their resorts defaced the natural landscape. In addition, in an attempt to "improve" the look of the park, trees were being logged, and there was talk of running a railway line through the most scenic areas of Yellowstone.

The park was an ecological disaster in the making, and as president of the Boone & Crockett Club, Teddy decided it was time to do something about it. On his return from the trip west, Teddy spurred the club on to start pressuring politicians in Washington to pass legislation that would properly protect the natural landscape of Yellowstone and future national parks.

Back in Washington, Teddy found himself busier than ever. The Civil Service Commission was vastly understaffed, making it difficult for the department to fully enforce the provisions of the Pendleton Act. Undeterred, Teddy pressed on relentlessly. He continued to butt heads with those who wanted to preserve the spoils system, and in particular with John Wanamaker.

In November things went badly for the Republicans in the congressional elections. As a result of a very unpopular tariff passed into law by the Congress in the previous session, voters decided it was time for a change and elected the largest Democratic majority in history to the House of Representatives. It was a bitter blow for the Republicans, and given the president's unpopularity, Teddy began to have doubts that Benjamin Harrison would be reelected in two years' time.

On August 13, 1891, Edith gave birth to a third child, a daughter whom they named Ethel. Teddy was delighted, and the growing family moved into a bigger house at 1215 Nineteenth Street NW in Washington.

While Teddy continued in his battle to institute civil-service reform in Washington, another crisis loomed on the horizon for him. This time it involved his brother, Elliot. For a while after his marriage to Anna, Elliot had stopped drinking. But slowly the old habit had returned, and Elliot sank firmly into the grip of alcoholism. Eventually Anna took the three children, Eleanor, Elliot Jr., and baby Hall, and left her husband, who continued to drink heavily. Finally Teddy decided he had to act. He feared that Elliot would squander all the money he had inherited on alcohol, leaving his wife and children nothing to live on. Teddy visited his brother and eventually convinced Elliot to sign over his estate to Anna and the children.

Eighteen ninety-two was a presidential election year. The Democrats nominated Grover Cleveland as their candidate to run against President Benjamin Harrison. As Teddy had feared, the campaign did not go well for Harrison, and on November 8, Cleveland beat him in the election.

Since Teddy was a Republican and the new president a Democrat, he supposed his days in Washington as a Civil Service commissioner were over. As he pondered what to do next, news reached Teddy that his sister-in-law Anna had died of diphtheria at age twenty-nine. Because of Elliot's alcoholism, the children went to live with Anna's mother, who was made their legal guardian.

Much to Teddy's surprise, his days in Washington were not yet over. President Cleveland was committed to civil-service reform, and he invited Teddy to stay on as a Civil Service commissioner. Teddy gladly accepted, and soon he was back at work fighting corruption and the spoils system. This time, though, he found himself locking heads with Democratic supporters of the spoils system. However, unlike Benjamin Harrison, the new president did not just mouth the words of reform; he gave more active support to the work of the Civil Service Commission, though the going was still tough for Teddy and the other commissioners.

On April 10, 1894, Edith gave birth to her fourth child, another son, who was named Archibald Bulloch Roosevelt. Despite the joy at the arrival of their new son, with five children in the house to care for, the Roosevelts' finances were stretched to the breaking point. As he stared bankruptcy in the face, Teddy decided to sell off several acres of land at Sagamore Hill to help defray the family's living expenses.

Eighteen ninety-four also saw the passage by Congress of the Park Protection Act. Teddy was delighted by this outcome; it was what he and the Boone & Crockett Club had worked hard for. Now, finally, the magnificent environment of Yellowstone National Park had the kind of protection from exploitation that it needed if it was to be enjoyed by future generations.

On Monday, August 13, 1894, as Teddy sat behind his desk busily working, a telegraph arrived from New York City informing him that his brother, Elliot, was gravely ill. The following day he received the news that Elliot had suffered an epileptic fit and died. Despite Teddy's disdain for his brother's drinking, he rushed to New York, grief stricken at the news. And when he saw the body of his younger brother, he wept uncontrollably.

As 1894 drew to a close, Teddy was becoming restless. His job as a Civil Service commissioner, while still demanding, ceased to challenge him as it once had. Teddy decided it was time for a change. The opportunity for such a change came when William L. Strong, the newly elected mayor of New York City, offered Teddy a seat on the Board of Police Commissioners for the city. Teddy gladly accepted the new position and left Washington for New York.

For the next two years Teddy threw himself into the job as enthusiastically and tirelessly as he had done when he was made a Civil Service commissioner. Once again he was hot on the trail of corruption, this time within the New York City Police

Department. As he soon discovered, there was much corruption within the department to fight.

After two years on the Board of Police Commissioners, Teddy was ready for another change, and this time the change would lead him back to Washington.

April 19, 1897, found Teddy Roosevelt climbing around the Navy Department's storage room looking for furniture for his new office. He had just been appointed the Assistant Secretary of the Navy, and he wanted a desk that reflected his new position. At the back of the room, he found a huge mahogany desk with ships carved on the desk doors. When Teddy learned that it had been used by one of his Civil War heroes, he knew it was the desk for him.

That afternoon the desk was moved into Teddy's freshly painted office. Teddy had it positioned so that he could swivel his chair and look out onto the White House lawns and gardens, a very satisfactory view in his opinion.

The position of Assistant Secretary of the Navy had opened up after William McKinley was elected president five months before. With his interest in naval warfare and strong record of public service and government management, Teddy wanted the job, but it had been a struggle to convince the new president to give the position to him. President McKinley and many of his advisers thought that Teddy was overly eager to prove that the navy could hold its own in a fight and that Teddy might be too easily challenged to go to war just to show how strong the navy was. However, after much lobbying, Teddy now found himself seated at his new desk as well as at a new set of challenges.

The current naval fleet consisted of six battleships and forty-eight other vessels, ranging from torpedo boats to armored cruisers. Five more battleships were under construction, but their progress had been held up because of lack of funds from Congress. Teddy thought that it was very shortsighted for a great country like the United States to have such a pitiful navy. Great Britain, France, Germany, and Russia had much larger navies, and Japan's navy was growing rapidly following its victory over China. Unless a strong navy was built up, all Teddy could see ahead was doom for the American people. Without a powerful navy, the United States would be more vulnerable to attacks by other countries.

Not everyone in Washington, including the president and Secretary of the Navy, John Long, agreed with Teddy's assessment. But Teddy was sure that the opportunity would come to convince the American people that they had to act. He knew that Long was a rather mild-mannered man who hated details, politics, and Washington summers. As a result Long left the capital for extended periods of time, leaving Teddy completely in charge of any situations that came up in his absence. Teddy figured that sooner or later some situation would arise while he was in charge that would allow him to expose the need for a strong navy.

To ease the stress of his new job, Teddy would often visit his sister Bamie and her new husband.

Much to everyone's surprise, Bamie had married two years before. She was forty, and her husband was a divorced forty-eight-year-old naval attaché named William Cowles. The couple lived near the White House, and Teddy was always welcome in their home.

As he assumed his new position, Teddy became particularly concerned about three situations. The first was the situation in Cuba, where Spain was using her strength to squash a local rebellion against Spanish rule. The second was Hawaii, which Teddy feared would soon be conquered by the Japanese unless the United States annexed it first. His third concern was a need for a canal across the Central American isthmus so that American ships could get from the Atlantic to the Pacific Ocean without having to sail around Cape Horn at the tip of South America. Teddy thought the best place for such a canal would be in Nicaragua, and he quietly set about drawing plans for it there.

While he worked away, Teddy waited to see how the summer of 1897 would unfold. He knew he was in a very delicate situation. Neither John Long nor the president agreed with his views about the navy. Instead of talking about actual fighting, Teddy concentrated on popularizing the idea that a great nation should be ready and able to fight at any time. In June he spoke to the Naval War College. In his address he pointed out:

> If we forget that in the last resort we can only secure peace by being ready and willing

> to fight for it, we may some day have bitter cause to realize that a rich nation which is slothful, timid, or unwieldy is an easy prey for any people which still retains those most valuable of all qualities, the soldierly virtues.... Cowardice in a race, as in an individual, is the unpardonable sin.... We ask for a great navy, partly because we think that the possession of such a navy is the surest guaranty of peace, and partly because we feel that no national life is worth having if the nation is not willing, when the need shall arise, to stake everything on the supreme arbitrament of war, and to pour out its blood, its treasure, and tears like water rather than to submit to the loss of honor and renown.... No triumph of peace is quite so great as the supreme triumphs of war.

As the summer progressed, Teddy began to see where a war might be necessary. The situation in Cuba had become more desperate as the Spanish gathered thousands of peasants who were calling for independence into camps where they could be watched night and day. This policy was called *reconcentrado*, and it proved to be a disaster. Food and medicine were in short supply, the water was bad, and diseases spread like wildfire through the camps.

This problem so close to home became a situation Teddy could not ignore. Liberating Cuba, rather than protecting Hawaii or building the canal, became his main aim. In his opinion, for the nation to be safe, it was crucial for the United States to show the world that it would not be threatened in the Western Hemisphere. Teddy explained himself in a letter to a friend: "I believe that [the president] ought now to recognize Cuba's independence and interfere, sending our fleet promptly to Havana. There would not in my opinion be very serious fighting; and what loss we encountered would be thrice over repaid by the ultimate results of our actions."

Slowly and methodically Teddy set about convincing the president that a war to liberate Cuba from Spain was in the best interests of the United States. He drew up a plan whereby most of the American fleet would assemble at Key West while a smaller fleet would gather in the Pacific to stop the Spanish from sending their Philippines-based fleet to join in the fight. Then, he proposed, ground troops should be sent into Cuba, with the navy backing them up.

All this planning put more pressure on President McKinley, but it was deflated in October 1897 when the Spanish government announced that it would disband the *reconcentrados* and move Cuba toward some form of independence. As an act of goodwill, the American and Spanish governments agreed to allow one of each country's naval vessels into each other's waters. The United States planned to send the USS *Maine* on a friendly visit to Havana, while the Spanish prepared to send one of their ships to the United States.

Teddy was not sure that this was a good move, but he was not asked his opinion, and like millions of other Americans, he waited to see what would happen. Meanwhile he made a rare visit back to New York to visit his family and be present for the birth of his and Edith's fifth child, another son, whom they named Quentin. Quentin was a strong, healthy baby like the others, but this time Edith did not make a quick recovery after the birth. She had some kind of stomach trouble, though none of the doctors who examined her could decide exactly what it was. Teddy was concerned about his wife, but he felt duty bound to get back to Washington. He left Edith and Quentin in the hands of other family members and returned to the capital city.

During the first week of February 1898, the USS *Maine* entered Havana Harbor and docked without incident. The Cuban people welcomed the vessel, and tours were given of it. However, on the night of February 15, something went terribly wrong. A huge explosion rocked Havana Harbor, sending red-hot debris high into the air as smoke billowed in all directions. When the smoke finally cleared, the USS *Maine* was a pile of wreckage lying at the bottom of the harbor. Two hundred sixty sailors aboard the ship were killed in the blast.

News of the sinking of the *Maine* electrified the United States, causing Teddy to call for an immediate war. After all, he argued, hadn't Spain already started it by luring an American naval vessel into Cuban waters and then blowing it up? To many it was a convincing argument but, as Teddy's opponents pointed out, not one he could prove. No one knew for sure what had caused the *Maine* to explode and sink. It could have been a bomb planted by the Spanish or some lone bomber, or it could have been an accidental engine explosion aboard the ship.

An investigation into the sinking was called for, but Teddy did not wait for the results of the investigation. He believed that the Spanish had deliberately sunk the *Maine* and that war was at hand. Since Navy Secretary Long was away on medical leave, Teddy acted alone, putting the Navy Department into high gear working around the clock to prepare for war.

With the apparent bombing of an American navy vessel by the Spanish, the American public swung around to Teddy's point of view, calling for Spain to be dealt with swiftly for daring to do such a thing. Eventually President McKinley had to agree, and he sent an ultimatum to the Spanish government: either give up Cuba or go to war. The Spanish, fearing a revolt at home if they gave up one of their colonies, decided not to give up Cuba.

While this situation was playing itself out, Teddy had matters at home to be concerned about. Edith was sicker than ever, but finally a doctor from Johns Hopkins Hospital diagnosed the problem. Edith had a stomach tumor that had to be operated on immediately. It was a risky operation, but Edith was near death, and Teddy had little option but to do whatever he could to try to save his wife's life. The children were dispatched to various relatives, and the operation was performed. Edith's life hung in the balance for two weeks before she began to make a slow recovery.

As Teddy tried to deal with the family crisis, he continued pushing hard for war with Spain. Then on April 11, 1898, almost a year to the day since Teddy had taken up his position as Assistant Secretary of the Navy, President McKinley asked Congress to authorize a war. "In the name of humanity," the president began, "in the name of civilization, in behalf of endangered American interests which give us the right and the duty to speak and to act...." Satisfied, Teddy watched silently as the president laid out his case.

The stage was set for war, and Teddy Roosevelt knew where he needed to be—right in the middle of it.

Chapter 13

Rough Riders

President McKinley gasped when Teddy told him he wanted to resign his position as Assistant Secretary of the Navy so that he could go and fight in the impending war with Spain. Teddy knew it seemed ludicrous to many for a man of his position to volunteer for the war along with the tens of thousands of "common" young men who were eager to fight. But he did not care. He might be thirty-nine years old, but ever since his father had bought himself out of the Civil War draft, Teddy had been wanting to go to war himself.

Finally he convinced the president that he was serious, and with McKinley's help, Teddy landed the perfect position, lieutenant colonel in the First Volunteer Cavalry under the command of his friend Leonard Wood. This cavalry was made up of three very different types of men. The first were hard-living cowboys from the territories of Arizona, New Mexico, Oklahoma, and the so-called Indian Territory. The second group comprised eastern volunteers, young men who had gone to universities such as Yale, Princeton, and Harvard, men who were used to riding polo ponies or galloping along on foxhunts. Reservation Indians made up the third group.

The three groups, 760 cowboys, 20 Indians, and 120 university students and graduates, met in San Antonio, Texas, in the middle of May 1898. There, in the shadow of the Alamo, they were to spend the coming weeks training together and molding themselves into a fighting force.

Since the war had not yet begun, the press focused its attention on the First Volunteer Cavalry regiment, whom reporters soon dubbed the "Rough Riders." As they watched the men train, the reporters were unanimous in agreeing on one thing: if there was one man who could knit three very different groups of men together into a single and cohesive fighting unit, it was Teddy Roosevelt, the man born into a privileged East Coast family but who had spent much time out west roaming the Badlands on horseback.

When Teddy saw the group of volunteers as they lined up for the first time in San Antonio, even he had doubts that the Rough Riders would ever become a team. But as the men trained together from five in the morning until nine at night, he worked hard at bridging the gap between the groups, gradually getting them to trust each other and accept each other as equals. His efforts paid off, and at the end of their training, the Rough Riders were a topnotch fighting force.

The people of San Antonio, at first standoffish, had warmed to the men training in their midst. They had mingled with them in bars and saloons and on the streets of town, and when it came time for the First Volunteer Cavalry to leave the city, they threw a going-away party. As part of the festivities, an outdoor band concert was held. Professor Carl Beck, a respected member of the German-American community in Texas, conducted the band. The band gave a spirited performance that delighted the Rough Riders and the gathered crowd of San Antonio citizens.

For their finale the band struck up a rousing march, which culminated in a thundering percussive crescendo. To enhance the effect of the crescendo, Professor Beck had arranged for a cannon to be fired three times in quick succession. Unfortunately he had neglected to inform the Rough Riders of this. When they heard the cannon fire, several of the men concluded that they were under attack, perhaps from a group of Spanish-sympathizing Mexicans. They drew their pistols and began firing wildly into the darkness, while two men raced forward to protect Professor Beck.

Soon other members of the Rough Riders joined in as a hail of bullets rained into the darkness. Meanwhile, the startled residents of San Antonio dived for cover wherever they could find it. Much to

Teddy's relief, order was eventually restored, and while many people's nerves were frayed, no one was injured in the melee.

The following morning the Rough Riders loaded themselves onto a train for the trip to Tampa, Florida, where the troops going to fight in Cuba were gathering. The horses were loaded into the rear cars of the train, and the men into the front. For four days the train rumbled along. In the evenings the train stopped and the men unloaded the horses to feed and water them.

When the men got to Tampa, the city was teeming with over thirty thousand soldiers who had gathered there from various training camps around the country. Tampa Bay was crowded with transport ships ready to ferry the men to Cuba.

A pleasant surprise awaited Teddy in Tampa. Friends in Washington had alerted Edith to the fact that her husband would be passing through the town on his way to Cuba. Recovered from her surgery, Edith had made the trek from New York to Florida to visit her husband. Teddy was delighted to see her, and Leonard Wood allowed Teddy to spend the next few nights at a local hotel with Edith.

After four days together, it was time for Edith to return to Sagamore Hill. Teddy escorted her to the train station and kissed her good-bye, but not before Edith had checked to see that her husband had sewn the twelve spare pairs of spectacles she had brought for him inside his uniform. There was no way Teddy could fight without his glasses, and he wanted to be well prepared with another pair close at hand in case he lost the ones he was wearing on the battlefield.

Teddy found the chaos in Tampa frustrating. In a letter he noted, "No words could describe to you the confusion and lack of system and the general mismanagement of affairs here." Food and medicine were in short supply, and orders more often than not were confusing or contradictory. Teddy experienced the latter firsthand when orders arrived for the Rough Riders to board a transport ship for Cuba. He soon learned that the Rough Riders and two other units had been ordered to board the same ship. The trouble was that there was room onboard for only one of the units, and Teddy decided it was going to be the Rough Riders. He raced to where his men were housed and ordered them to follow him as he led them through the crowded city to the docks, where their transport ship was just berthing.

No sooner had the gangplank been lowered from the vessel than the Rough Riders charged aboard. When the other two units arrived to board the ship according to their orders, they found the vessel full. The Rough Riders smiled and patted Teddy on the back and congratulated him on his quick thinking in getting them onto the ship first. They had already left the dock when Teddy was informed that only a few of the horses had been loaded onboard the ship. The Rough Riders had been turned into Rough Marchers!

The men were not so grateful a week later when the transport ship was still bobbing at anchor in

Tampa Bay. News had reached Washington that a fleet of Spanish warships was lying in wait in the Straits of Florida, which separated Florida from Cuba. It was doubtful that the report was true, but cautious politicians in Washington ordered the ships to lie at anchor until things could be checked out. Instead of sailing away to Cuba, the Rough Riders rocked back and forth on their transport ship in Tampa Bay. The weather was humid, making it almost impossible to stay inside the ship during the heat of the day. The men piled out onto the deck, only to be met by the putrid odor of the raw sewage that ran directly into the bay from the overcrowded city.

Finally the order to set sail was given. The powers that be in the Navy Department and the War Department in Washington were convinced that no Spanish ships were lying in wait for them. Slowly the column of forty-eight transport ships and battleships steamed out of Tampa Bay and into the Gulf of Mexico, where they headed south and then east. They sailed along the coast of Cuba until they came to Daiquiri, located on the southeast coast, where the American forces planned to land on the beach. But before they could land, two of the U.S. battleships pounded the beach and surrounding area with shells from their massive guns. A group of Spanish soldiers had begun firing at the fleet from the beach, but it did not take too many shells from the battleships to send them into retreat.

It was time to disembark on their invasion of Cuba, but the transport ships had no dock to pull into. Instead the men had to clamber over the sides of the ships and into the water, carrying their rifles, ammunition, and heavy packs with them. Once in the water, they had to scramble through the surf for the beach. At the same time, what horses and mules had been transported on the ships were driven overboard into the ocean in the hope they would swim to shore. Soon the surf was teeming with soldiers, horses, and mules. Many of the horses and mules became disoriented in the water. Some swam from ship to ship before becoming exhausted and drowning. Others made it almost to shore before being spooked by the crashing waves and turning around and swimming in the opposite direction out to sea. By the time the landing was over, the carcasses of many horses and mules had washed ashore and littered the beach. In the mayhem of the landing, two soldiers also were drowned.

Once on the beach, the men dried themselves and their equipment in the sun. They slept the night in the open on the beach. The following morning Teddy ordered the men to build lean-tos from palm fronds to provide them some protection from the burning Caribbean sun.

The first objective of the American troops was to capture the town of Santiago de Cuba, located fifteen miles northwest of Daiquiri. Santiago was home to the Spanish Caribbean fleet. The fleet was at anchor in the harbor, and the Americans hoped that by blockading the harbor and capturing the town they could demoralize the Spanish early in the fight. A day after landing on the beach, General William Shafter, commander of the American forces in Cuba, ordered the men to advance on Santiago.

As the throng of troops moved inland from the beach, Teddy and Leonard Wood were determined not to miss the fight. Because the Rough Riders were at the back of the column of soldiers, Teddy and Leonard marched their horseless soldiers hard to get to the head of the long column of troops. The swift march was demanding on the men, who were used to riding. As the day wore on and the hot sun baked down, the packs the men carried seemed to get heavier and heavier until they felt like an unbearable burden. While sympathetic to their situation, Teddy kept the men moving. If there was going to be a battle, the Rough Riders were going to be in the thick of it.

Teddy and his men made it to the front of the column, and the next day at Las Guásimas, on the road to Santiago, they engaged a group of Spanish soldiers. The firefight ended when the Spanish soldiers retreated. In a letter home to his sister Conie, Teddy described the skirmish.

> We struck the Spaniards and had a brisk fight for 2 1/2 hours before we drove them out of their position. We lost a dozen men killed or mortally wounded, and sixty severely or slightly wounded. One man was killed as he stood beside a tree with me. Another bullet went through a tree behind

> which I stood and filled my eyes with bark. The last charge I led on the left using a rifle I took from a wounded man....The fire was very hot at one or two points where the men around me went down like ninepins.

Following the skirmish, the Rough Riders spent a very uncomfortable night in the open. They were exhausted from the hard marching and the fighting, and because they had marched so fast to get to the head of the column, their baggage, which included tents to sleep in and more food, had not yet caught up with them. Still, Teddy went to sleep that night strangely satisfied that he was finally in the thick of a war.

A grim sight greeted Teddy when he arose in the morning. Hundreds of vultures had descended on the bodies of the dead Spanish soldiers and were slowly devouring them. Teddy hoped that in the course of the war he would not meet such an end. But if he must die for the cause of freedom, he was prepared to do so.

General Shafter had intended to quickly push on to Santiago. After the skirmish at Las Guásimas, however, he decided to wait a few days to allow his troops, strung out in a long line, to catch up to the advance guard. It was a frustrating wait for Teddy and the Rough Riders. The tropical heat and humidity were stifling, and the mosquitoes bit the men mercilessly. And having begun, the men were eager to press on and finish the fight. Yet with so few provisions, Teddy also realized that it was wise to wait and let their supply chain catch up with them, despite the hardship.

Finally, on June 30, 1898, the order to move out came. The men lumbered their packs onto their backs, took up the weapons, and began the march forward. The road they followed led them through thick, tropical jungle that seemed to disorient and make many of the Rough Riders from the plains claustrophobic. These men were used to wide-open spaces where they could see for miles, not the dense jungle that now closed in around them. Also, the heat was so intense that many of the men began to suffer the effects of exhaustion and dehydration. Finally, well after the sun had gone down, the Rough Riders stopped and camped for the night on the side of El Pozo hill.

As the sun rose the next morning, Teddy took in the view. The side of the hill they were on sloped down into a narrow valley, and another hill rose gently on the other side. But the tranquility of the scene was soon shattered when American artillery opened fire on the Spanish positions across the valley. The Spanish fired back, and Teddy quickly realized that he and the Rough Riders were caught between the fire. Spanish shells soon began to fall around them, showering the men with deadly shrapnel. When a piece of shrapnel ripped open his tunic and grazed his arm, Teddy knew he had to get his men to cover. Quickly he ordered them to follow him as he led the way up El Pozo hill to shelter on the other side, out of the range of Spanish artillery fire.

No sooner had the men made it over the crown of the hill than they were ordered to move to the right and link up with another army unit. The Rough Riders set out as fast as they could. Spanish gunfire rained down on them as they forded the San Juan River. On the other side of the river, a road ran through a narrow valley. On the left side of the valley was San Juan Hill, and on the right, Kettle Hill, which the soldiers had named after the old sugar-refining kettle that lay at the top of the hill. Spanish forces were dug in on both hills, and they fired ceaselessly with their superior German Mauser rifles at the American soldiers.

Teddy was unsure what his orders were now that they were across the river and under heavy fire. Already several of the Rough Riders had been cut down by enemy fire. Teddy summoned a messenger to go back across the river and find out if they were to attack the Spanish positions head-on. As the messenger stood to salute Teddy, he was killed by a Spanish bullet and fell forward into Teddy's arms.

Teddy quickly dispatched another messenger, but when he could not find a ranking officer to give the order for the Rough Riders to attack, he decided that if he did not act quickly, his men could all be dead before the order to attack came. He was about to order his men to attack under his own authority when a breathless messenger raced up with the official order to attack.

Teddy wasted no time. He ordered the men to charge. With a deafening yell they surged forward, with Teddy in the lead. As they raced up the slope of Kettle Hill, other army units joined the fight from other directions. Bullets sprayed down on them like lead rain, but the men kept running forward. Within minutes they had reached the crest of the low hill. Totally outnumbered and overwhelmed, the Spanish troops fled, leaving the hill to the Americans. As the American soldiers began to celebrate their victory, bullets and artillery fire began to rain down on them again, this time from the Spanish forces entrenched on San Juan Hill. The men dived for cover and began to return fire.

When Teddy saw American troops begin to storm San Juan Hill, he ordered the Rough Riders to follow him as he charged back down Kettle Hill and up San Juan Hill. The Spanish kept firing at the approaching American soldiers, but they were outnumbered fifteen to one. Eventually they, too, gave up the fight and fled toward Santiago, a mile away. Teddy and the Rough Riders arrived at the top of the hill in time to overrun the positions of a number of the Spanish troops who were too slow in fleeing.

The Battle of San Juan Hill was soon over, and much to his relief, although tired and battle sore, Teddy was invigorated by the whole affair. Other members of the Rough Riders, however, did not live to see victory. The unit had suffered heavy casualties in the battle.

Chapter 14

Vice President

The battle was over but not the war. Teddy followed its progress as best he could, though he was constantly frustrated by the lack of information that was passed on to him. How he wished he knew what was happening in the War Department in Washington.

One piece of news that did travel fast was that, following the Battle of San Juan Hill, Admiral Pascual Cervera, commander of the Spanish fleet, decided to flee Cuba rather than have his ships bombed by American artillery. He loaded up his six warships and headed out of the harbor, right into the arms of the waiting American fleet. Within hours all six ships either had run aground or were sunk. It was a decisive victory in Cuba, and Teddy was anxious for his Rough Riders to be shipped out to the next assignment, which he assumed would be the island of Puerto Rico. However, day after day the troops sat outside Santiago. Teddy concluded that the War Department had more important things to do at that moment than evacuate troops from Cuba.

At first being stuck in Cuba was merely an inconvenience, but it soon turned into a disaster. Teddy watched helplessly as his men came down with cholera, malaria, and other illnesses related to their infected wounds. Then cases of yellow fever were reported, which created a whole new problem for the troops left behind in Cuba. The United States government feared that the soldiers would bring the disease back to the mainland and ordered the troops to stay there until the fever ran its course. This made Teddy angrier than anything had ever before made him. These were his men. They had served their country well, and now they were being abandoned. He wrote letters to everyone he knew in Washington until he finally pressured the War Department into action.

In early August the Rough Riders were finally evacuated from Cuba. They did not get their wish to join another fight. Instead, they were shipped off to Montauk, at the eastern tip of Long Island, to be quarantined.

On the way to Montauk, Teddy received a telegraph message from Washington that the Spanish-American War, as it was being called, was officially over. The United States had won the day. Cuba was now independent, and the Philippines, Guam, and

Puerto Rico had been ceded to the United States. Teddy's remarkable but short career as a soldier was over.

The quarantine on Long Island lasted for five days. On the final day several of Teddy's men asked him to come with them. Teddy followed them outside, where he found his regiment standing around the perimeter of the camp's quadrangle. Surrounding the men were the black troops of the Ninth and Tenth Cavalries and the hospital staff who were supervising their quarantine. In the middle of the quadrangle was a makeshift table bearing a large object that had been covered with a horse blanket.

Teddy was led into the middle of his men. Tears filled his eyes as he realized this would probably be the last time he saw them all together.

Trooper Will Murphy cleared his throat and addressed Teddy. "Colonel Roosevelt," he began, "the First Volunteer Cavalry regiment wishes to present you with a small token of our admiration, love, and esteem." With that, Will pulled the blanket off the object, which turned out to be a two-foot-high casting of Frederic Remington's statue *Bronco Buster.*

As Teddy studied the statue of a cowboy mounted on a rearing pony, he smiled. It was the perfect gift from a group of Rough Riders. He struggled to find the right words to say. "I am proud of this regiment beyond measure. It is primarily an American regiment, and it is American because it is composed of all the races which have made America their country.... To have such a gift from this peculiarly American regiment touches me more than I can say. It is something I shall hand down to my children." Then he looked at the black soldiers who were watching. Many of them had risked their lives on San Juan Hill as well. To them he said, "Between you and the other cavalry regiments there is a tie which we trust will never be broken." He took a deep breath. "Now, I would like to shake the hand of every one of my Rough Riders, and thank you for your valiant service to our country."

His good-byes complete, Teddy returned to his tent to make preparations for his trip home to Sagamore Hill. He was not sure what lay ahead for him, but he had some strong suspicions. For his gallantry at San Juan Hill, the newspapers lauded him as a war hero fresh from the battlefield. It was not long before U.S. Senator Tom Platt, leader of the New York Republican party, nominated Teddy for governor of New York. Although Platt was not particularly fond of Teddy, the Republican party needed a winning candidate in the upcoming election, and with all the public adulation, Teddy was a winning candidate.

Teddy's campaign for governor took on a circus atmosphere, as he invited some of the Rough Riders to travel with him. He also brought along an army bugler and reminded his audiences that he had listened to the sound of the bugle in the tropics as he served his country.

Even so, the campaign was a hard-fought one. Nearly one and one-third million votes were cast, and when they were tallied, Teddy had won the election by less than eighteen thousand votes.

Six months before, he had been a cavalry officer charging up San Juan Hill; now he was governor of the most populous state in the country.

Shortly after the election he wrote to his friend Cecil Rice, explaining, "I have played it in bull luck this summer. First, to get into the war; then to get out of it; then to get elected. I have worked hard all my life, and have never been particularly lucky, but this summer I was lucky and am enjoying life to the full. I know perfectly well that the luck will not continue, and it is not necessary that it should. I am more than contented to be Governor of New York, and shall not care if I never hold another office."

Two weeks later Teddy was wondering just how lucky he was. Senator Platt had thrown considerable support behind Teddy to get him elected. Now he wanted to have his say in how Teddy ran the state of New York. He came to Teddy one day and handed him a telegram from a man named Francis Hendricks. The telegram said that Hendricks was accepting the position as the new superintendent of public works. The only problem was that Teddy had not offered the post to Francis Hendricks. Tom Platt had done that without even telling Teddy what he was up to.

The battle lines were clearly drawn. Senator Platt wanted Teddy to rubber-stamp his choices for new positions in the state government, and Teddy, who had run on a platform of eradicating corruption, wanted to make his own decisions based on what he thought was best for the state.

It was a tense moment. Teddy knew it was a dangerous move to challenge a man like Tom Platt, who wielded so much power within the Republican party, but he felt he had no choice. He told the senator that he would have to withdraw his offer to Hendricks because it was not his offer to make. Teddy was the governor, and it was his job to select and appoint the most qualified person.

Senator Platt was unwilling to take no for an answer, and he pulled all sorts of strings to humiliate Teddy into allowing Hendricks to be the new superintendent of public works. Teddy, for his part, set about finding a man he thought was right for the job. This was no easy task, because every qualified person he approached refused to even consider the job. Senator Platt had gotten to them first and made it clear that they should not accept the position.

It was quite an impasse, but Teddy refused to back down. Eventually he drew up a list of four men he felt were suitable for the job and allowed Platt to choose one man from that list. Now both men were satisfied, and they could continue with their work.

This was the first of many compromises Teddy made with Senator Platt. The senator was able to say he had made the selection of various posts, while Teddy knew that a well-qualified person had been appointed and that no one was appointed as a reward for something he had done for a politician.

Teddy had many more battles with Senator Platt, but he had not backed down in his first confrontation, and he did not back down in subsequent confrontations. Nor did he back down from his idea that the government existed to serve the people. To prove that he meant it, Teddy did something no other politician—mayor, governor, or senator—had ever done before. He opened his work to the press. Every day that he was in his office, he held two fifteen-minute press conferences, one in the morning and one in the afternoon. The newspaper reporters would troop into his office, and Teddy would perch on the end of his desk, answering any questions the men threw at him. The reporters were understandably delighted with this new access to someone in power, and a reporter for the *New York Times* noted that "[Teddy] has torn down the curtain that shut in the Governor and taken the public into his confidence." That was just the kind of thing Teddy loved to hear.

By the end of the first legislative session, Teddy had racked up an impressive list of accomplishments. He had raised salaries for teachers, banned the segregation of public schools by race, preserved the Palisades in New York City, prevented the dumping of commercial waste in the streams of the Adirondack and Catskill Mountains, and introduced new civil-service laws.

At the end of the session, Teddy spent the first half of the summer on a tour of the West, including a reunion of his Rough Riders, before settling back at Sagamore Hill with his family. Being with the family, however, proved more trying than he had imagined. Alice, now fifteen years old, was quite out of hand. She was willful and headstrong, and if either Teddy or Edith tried to make her do anything she did not want to do, she would threaten to do something disgraceful in public. Teddy could only sigh. How different she was from her mother.

Something else was on Teddy's mind that summer: the vice presidency of the United States. Teddy's old friend Henry Cabot Lodge had suggested that Teddy put his name forward for vice president to run with William McKinley in the presidential election of 1900. As Teddy mulled it over, he came up with three reasons why it would never work. First, the vice presidency did not pay enough to make ends meet. His salary as a governor was ten thousand dollars a year, and the vice president got only eight thousand dollars and had to pay for his own housing in Washington on top of that. Second, he did not want to leave New York. He knew he was doing a good job as governor, and he wanted to see it through to the end of his term. Third and most important, William McKinley already had a future running mate, the current vice president, Garret Hobart. That is, until November 21, 1899, when Hobart died unexpectedly.

Nonetheless, Teddy's other two reasons were enough to keep him from wanting the job. But without warning, Teddy was thrust into the national spotlight anyway. Senator Tom Platt endlessly promoted the idea that Teddy would be the ideal running mate for William McKinley. It took Teddy a few weeks to work out why: the senator wanted him out of New York. Teddy had changed too many things for Senator Platt's liking, and the senator wanted him moved out of Albany to anywhere, even Washington, D.C.

Although Teddy did all he could to tell people he was not interested in the job, support for him grew stronger. In fact, all of his talk about not wanting the job only made him seem humble and perfect for the job of vice president.

Teddy finally gave in, and on June 19, 1900, he was officially nominated as the vice-presidential candidate on the Republican ticket. Political pollsters were giving the Republican candidates a two-to-one chance of victory over the Democratic challengers.

Now that he was committed to the race, Teddy ran harder than just about anyone else ever had. Many people who came to hear him speak thought he should be running for president. He gave hundreds of speeches and covered twenty-one thousand miles of the American countryside.

By the time the election took place on November 6, 1900, the odds were up to five-to-one that William McKinley and Teddy would win. And so they did. It was the greatest Republican victory since 1872.

March 4, 1901, dawned an overcast day as Teddy prepared himself for the inauguration. Edith and the children sat proudly in the gallery of the Senate chamber as Teddy marched in, his head held high, his shoulders back, his frock coat buttoned tightly around him. Finally Teddy stepped forward to take the oath of office as vice president. Afterward he addressed the gathered crowd, explaining to them that great responsibilities came with the "great privileges and great powers" of America. "We belong to a young nation," he said, "already a giant strength, yet whose political strength is but a forecast of the power that is to come. We stand supreme in a continent, in a hemisphere. East and West we look across two great oceans toward the larger world life in which, whether we will or not, we must take an ever-increasing share."

After the swearing-in ceremony, Teddy rode with the president in the inaugural parade down Pennsylvania Avenue to the White House. It was a grand spectacle, which Edith and the children watched from a second-story balcony along the parade route.

Teddy had little to do immediately after the inauguration. The Senate sat for four days and then adjourned until December. Those were not four of Teddy's favorite days. It did not take long to confirm what he already knew: the job of vice president was very boring. He did not get to participate in any of the debates. He just had to sit quietly and listen, and he got to vote only if the Senate was tied. For someone who liked to talk as much as Teddy Roosevelt did, this was very difficult. Teddy wrote to his friend Cecil complaining that he felt like the fifth wheel on a coach.

Once the brief Senate session was over, Teddy returned to Sagamore Hill. All of the children were there except for Ted, who had just enrolled in school at Groton. Teddy read books, chopped wood, and took Edith for long rows in the boat on the bay. All in all, it was a perfect break before he took up his duties as vice president.

At the end of summer, both Teddy and President McKinley decided it would be a good idea for them to tour America. They went separately so they could cover more ground. Teddy started out in Vermont while the president went to the Pan American Exposition in Buffalo, New York. Even if the vice presidency was going to be boring, Teddy did enjoy traveling and meeting so many different people.

On September 6, 1901, Teddy was dressing for a reception when the telephone in his room rang. When he picked up the phone, he heard the most shocking news. President McKinley had been shot. He was not dead, but he had suffered a very serious wound. Teddy canceled the reception and immediately set out to be with the president.

A special train took Teddy to Buffalo, where he rushed to William McKinley's side. Teddy learned that the president had reached out to shake the hand of a supporter when the man produced a gun and shot him in the stomach. The man, a young Polish-American, had been captured and declared himself to be an anarchist.

Teddy looked down at the fifty-eight-year-old president. McKinley looked in good spirits, a fact that was soon confirmed by the doctor in attendance. The doctor explained to Teddy that the bullets had entered the president's stomach, torn holes in his liver and pancreas, and then lodged in his back. Despite this, the doctor hoped for a full recovery. As long as there was no infection and gangrene did not set in, a surgeon could repair the damage. The news was a tremendous relief to Teddy, who waited with the president during the operation.

Everything went well, and on September 10, four days after the shooting, the doctor assured Teddy that he could go on with his planned activities. These included a camping trip in the Adirondacks with Edith and the children. Teddy was glad to be out in the fresh air again, and he tried not to think of the possibility that another madman might be out there, ready to take a shot at *him*.

On September 13, Teddy and several other campers set out to climb Mount Marcy, the highest point of the Adirondacks. Even though he was nearly forty-three years old, Teddy could keep up with the youngest members of the group, despite the prediction of his doctor so many years ago that he had a weak heart that wouldn't endure any strain. The climbers soon reached the top of the mountain but were unable to see much from the summit because of the rainy weather. They did not linger long before setting off down the mountain again.

The group stopped at a small lake near the foot of the mountain to eat. Just as Teddy was about to take a bite of his sandwich, he spotted a young man running toward them. Goose bumps rose on the back of Teddy's neck. Instinctively Teddy knew that the runner was carrying bad news.

And he was. President McKinley had taken a turn for the worse, and Teddy needed to be at his side. Teddy's mind raced. He needed to get to a telephone, but as far as he could tell, the nearest one was twelve miles away. He set out on foot at a cracking pace, scarcely stopping to catch his breath as he went.

When Teddy finally got through to McKinley's doctor, the news was even worse. The president was dying. Teddy rushed back to his campsite to tell Edith and collect a few things. When he told his family the news, Quentin clung to his leg. "Don't go, Daddy," he begged. "If you become president, you will be shot too."

Teddy gently disentangled his youngest son and gave him a big hug. "I have to go. My country needs me," he said. Minutes later Teddy was off on a furious forty-mile wagon ride to North Creek Station, where a special train would meet him and take him to the president's side. The team of horses was changed three times on the way to the train station, and each time Teddy urged the driver to get every ounce of speed out of the new horses that he could.

Dawn was just breaking when Teddy arrived at North Creek Station. He jumped down from the wagon, luggage in hand, ready to board the train. But as he did so, someone handed him a folded piece of paper and a kerosene lamp. With trembling hands Teddy unfolded the telegram and read by the light of the lamp. "President McKinley died at 2:15 this morning. Come immediately."

Chapter 15

Accidental President

Teddy Roosevelt checked his watch; it was exactly three o'clock, September 14, 1901, and he was standing silently in Ansley Wilcox's home in Buffalo, New York. President McKinley lay dead in a room upstairs. Secretary of War Elihu Root, the most senior cabinet member present, had sent one of his aides to the local library to read old newspaper accounts of the induction of Chester Arthur following the assassination of President Garfield. When the aide returned, he was carrying several old newspapers that Root scanned quickly before announcing that it was time for the swearing-in ceremony.

Several reporters, along with Root, Judge Hazel, and a few other lower-ranking cabinet members, filed in to the Wilcox family library. In that somber atmosphere forty-two-year-old Theodore Roosevelt became the twenty-sixth president of the United States of America, the youngest man to hold the office.

After the somber ceremony, Teddy went for a walk. He needed time to take it all in. Two days before, he had been happily climbing a mountain and wondering how he would fill in his time as the vice president. Now he was the president. He thought back to the time when as small children he and Elliot had leaned out the window of their grandfather's house and watched President Abraham Lincoln's funeral procession pass by. Since then Teddy had lived through the assassination of two more presidents, and he was aware of the potential danger that lay ahead for him. However, he chose not to dwell on it. As a Rough Rider and a general adventurer, he had faced death before, and he knew it was a waste of his time to worry about what might happen to him in the future.

Edith joined Teddy for William McKinley's funeral, and then she returned to Sagamore Hill to continue packing. Meanwhile, on the morning of September 23, Teddy moved a few of his belongings into the White House. He spent the rest of the day signing papers. As he did so, he realized that this would have been his father's seventieth birthday. He took it as a good sign. Then, not wanting to be alone that evening, he invited Conie and Bamie to join him for dinner.

The White House butler served coffee after the meal and presented Teddy with a boutonniere: a little-known rose, a yellow saffronia, Teddy's father's personal favorite. As Teddy pinned the rose onto his lapel, he commented to his sisters, "I think there is a blessing connected with this."

And so there seemed to be. Teddy often felt his father's presence in the White House, especially when he had difficult decisions to make. He would often stop for a moment and ask himself what his father would do in such a circumstance and let the answer guide his own course.

One thing Teddy did that surprised most politicians was not to change everything President McKinley had set in motion. The other two "accidental" presidents, Andrew Johnson and Chester Arthur, had turned the plans of Abraham Lincoln and James Garfield on their heads. Teddy believed the country would be best served by continuing along the lines William McKinley had laid out. Besides, he reasoned, people were too upset by the assassination to place more stress and uncertainty on them by changing course for the country.

Two days after Teddy moved into the White House, Edith and the children arrived, along with a cook and two personal maids. Teddy was glad for the sense of order Edith brought to the house and for the liveliness of his children. There was never a dull moment, as the White House servants were soon to find out. There had not been so much mischief since the 1860s, when Abraham Lincoln's sons Tad and Willie ran wild in the White House halls.

The three youngest children, ten-year-old Ethel, seven-year-old Archie, and four-year-old Quentin, were particularly entertaining for the press to cover. Teddy could not help smiling when, just three days after they arrived, the three youngest children pulled a trick on the watchman lighting the streetlamps in the park across Pennsylvania Avenue. The children arrived in the park at dusk, just as the watchman, using a ladder, was lighting the lamps on one side of the park. When the watchman moved to the other side of the park, Ethel shinnied up the lampposts and turned off the lamps. On discovering that the lights he had just lit were now all out, the watchman scratched his head in utter bewilderment, much to the delight of the children.

The children also soon decided that the huge marble staircases of the White House were perfect for tobogganing down on trays borrowed from the kitchen and that the long, hardwood floors were perfect for roller-skating, bicycling, and walking on stilts. Still, nothing amused reporters as much as covering Archie's recovery from a bad case of measles. Quentin decided that the best cure for Archie was a visit from his pony. The children, with the aid of the White House coachman, smuggled the pony past the guards and ushers and into the elevator for a trip to Archie's second-floor bedroom. They were discovered on the way down in the elevator, but Quentin was unapologetic. He declared that the visit from the pony had been just the thing to perk his brother up. Teddy laughed heartily when he heard the story. His younger children certainly were a handful, but no more so than he had been as a child.

Meanwhile Alice was making quite a splash for herself in Washington. Tall, blonde, and very opinionated, she challenged Teddy as the most outspoken person in the family. Much to his chagrin, she took up smoking and bought herself a small automobile, which she drove alone. Neither Teddy nor Edith could do much to keep her under control, as she had an independent income from her Lee grandparents. This was enough to allow her to do or buy whatever she liked. The press soon dubbed her "Princess Alice," and her every move was the subject of gossip.

Four months after Teddy took office, Alice's debut was held at the White House. It was the first such party since that of President Grant's daughter Nellie, and it led to many heated discussions. Alice did not like the flooring in the room or the fact that her father insisted on punch rather than champagne. Nor did Teddy allow her to give away expensive favors to all of the guests. These things made Alice furious, and Teddy despaired that the two of them would ever understand each other. He much preferred the company of his niece Eleanor, who had returned from school in Europe in time to attend the party. Although she was no beauty, Eleanor had a concern for all classes of society, a trait Teddy would dearly have loved to see in his daughter.

The press had never been happier with the access they had to the president, and they eagerly covered the party and everything else that happened in the White House.

One thing that surprised, and angered, many people was that Teddy invited a black man to dine with him at the White House. It was the first time a president had ever done such a thing, and it caused a scandal. Teddy could not have cared less. He greatly admired Booker T. Washington, the founder of a vocational school in Tuskegee, Alabama, and valued his opinion on how to bring southern blacks into the Republican fold. In fact, Teddy had little time for racial divisions. He allowed Quentin to play with Roswell Pinckney, the son of a black White House steward, and the two little boys became best friends. When Teddy admitted that his children probably needed more attention than either he or Edith had time to provide, he hired a young black man named James Amos to be the children's supervisor. James proved to be a wonderful choice and was soon treated like a member of the family.

There were other controversies too, but they had to do with big-business legislation and the railroads. Teddy had always fought corruption, and now he had one of the biggest industrial businessmen in the world in his sights. The man was J. P. Morgan, who had brought together U.S. Steel, General Electric, and International Harvester into one enormously wealthy and powerful unit, or trust. Teddy was convinced that Morgan had violated federal laws concerning the control of three western railroads, the Great Northern, the Northern Pacific, and the Burlington Railroad. Now that he had a monopoly in the West, Morgan was using it to exploit manufacturers who needed freight moved. Teddy was determined to bring the facts of the case before the American people, and in February 1902 he ordered the Justice Department to file charges against Morgan's company, Northern Securities.

The action sent shock waves pulsing through Washington and Wall Street. The Morgans and the Roosevelts went back a long way. J. P. Morgan's father and Teddy's father had both been founders of the American Museum of Natural History and had sat on many other important boards together. It was unbelievable to J. P. Morgan and many other very wealthy men that Teddy could "turn on his own class" like this.

But turn he did. As a result, the stock market plunged while the common people cheered to see Teddy being fair to all classes. Teddy spent hours explaining to the press what he thought of these huge corporations, or trusts. He pointed out that he was not against all trusts. There were some good trusts, which offered good services at reasonable prices, but there were also bad trusts. Bad trusts used their size and power to beat down any opposition and then jacked up prices until they were so unreasonable that many people could not afford to pay them. But people had no alternatives because the trusts had seen to it that no one else succeeded in their market. These were the trusts that Teddy was determined to break.

Then, in May 1902, coal miners in eastern Pennsylvania went on strike, protesting the conditions under which they had to work. The miners worked twelve-hour shifts six days a week. For their labor they were paid an annual wage of $560, from which was deducted their rent, money to pay for oil for their lamps, and a compulsory charge for the company doctor. This left many miners in perpetual debt to the mining companies, which were mostly owned by the railroad companies, among them J. P. Morgan's company. Conditions in the mines were treacherous, and often children as young as ten were put to work there. The miners wanted the long shifts reduced to eight hours, a 10 to 20 percent pay increase, a fairer system for weighing the coal they produced, and recognition of their union. The mining companies had refused these demands, and so 150,000 miners went on strike.

The coal miners' strike was into its fourth month when Teddy visited Pittsfield, Massachusetts, on September 3. He was sitting in his carriage in Pittsfield when it was struck by a trolley car. The horses reared up, and everyone inside was flung from the carriage. The Secret Service man riding beside the coachman was instantly killed, and everyone else was injured. Teddy had a gash on his head and one on his left leg, but he insisted on continuing with his visit. A few days later his leg was sore and swollen. An abscess had developed in his leg, and Teddy agreed to have it operated on to prevent blood poisoning. The operation was only a partial success, and when he returned to Washington by special train, Teddy had a second operation. This time the surgeon scraped his shinbone to remove all of the infection. This operation was a success, but Teddy had to resign himself to a lifetime with an aching shinbone, especially when he got tired.

For several weeks after the operations, Teddy was restricted to a wheelchair, with which he managed to terrorize the staff as he raced it around the house like a chariot.

It was while he was still in the wheelchair that Teddy finally decided he had to do something about the miners' strike. As winter approached, coal was beginning to be in short supply, and in New York the price of a ton of coal had soared from five dollars to thirty dollars. Schools were being forced to close as they ran out of fuel for heating, and people everywhere were beginning to clamor for the strike to end.

Even though he was president, Teddy did not have the constitutional authority to intervene and settle the strike outright. However, he called representatives of the miners and mine owners to Washington for a meeting with him. At the meeting he pleaded for the two sides to settle their differences. The miners agreed to go back to work and have their case settled by an arbitration board, but the mine owners refused. Afterward Teddy was so incensed by the refusal of George Baer, the mine owners' representative, to submit the strike to arbitration that he fumed, "If it wasn't for the high office I hold, I would have taken [Baer] by the seat of the breeches and the nape of the neck and chucked him out of that window."

Teddy decided to take another tack. As president he felt he was the people's representative in the issue, and the strike now threatened the good of the people. Pushing his constitutional power as far as he could, he ordered ten thousand federal troops into Pennsylvania. If requested by the local authorities, the troops had orders to take over the mines and restore public order under Teddy's direct authority. The mine owners were shocked by this turn of events. They were not sure whether Teddy was bluffing, and they were unwilling to force the issue to find out. Under duress they agreed to submit the dispute to a board of arbitrators chosen by Teddy and the owners. Teddy made sure that at least one member of the board represented the interests of the miners, and the miners agreed to go back to work. The strike was over.

With the strike settled, in November 1902, Teddy decided he needed a break, so he arranged to go on a bear hunt in Mississippi. Game was very scarce on the hunt, and Teddy began to wonder if he would ever see a bear. Finally his dogs surrounded a small, scraggly black bear. The bear looked so pathetic that Teddy decided he would not shoot it. The following Saturday a cartoon about Teddy and the bear appeared in the *Washington Post* under the title "Drawing the Line in Mississippi."

When Teddy returned to the White House, a letter was waiting for him from a man who owned a toy store in Brooklyn, New York. The man had made a cuddly stuffed bear and wanted permission to call it a "Teddy Bear," after the incident in Mississippi.

Teddy thought the whole idea was a little odd, but he wrote back, "I don't think my name will mean much to the bear business, but you're welcome to use it." Soon every fashionable East Coast child owned a Teddy Bear of one sort or another.

Another issue reared its head at the end of 1902—a canal across the Central American isthmus. Teddy had been interested in this ever since he was Assistant Secretary of the Navy, and now Congress was interested in the issue as well. The thinking had been to build such a canal across Nicaragua, but a new possibility had presented itself. In 1878 a French company had obtained a concession from the Colombian government to dig a canal across the Colombian province of Panama. Work had begun on the project under the guidance of Ferdinand de Lesseps, who had built the Suez Canal. However, things did not go well for the project. There was a crippling shortage of money to build the canal as well as formidable engineering problems to overcome. Also, yellow fever had killed twenty-two thousand workers, and the project had been abandoned in 1889. Now the French company wanted to sell the concession and all of the earthmoving equipment still lying in the Panamanian jungle to the United States for forty million dollars.

Teddy was immediately interested. A canal across Panama would be much shorter than a canal across Nicaragua and thus would cost less to build. Teddy was eager to see a great canal linking the Atlantic and Pacific Oceans. Such a canal would help the United States protect itself on the seas in both the Atlantic and the Pacific. Teddy pushed Congress to approve the buyout of the French company, which it did.

Since Panama belonged to Colombia, Teddy sent Secretary of State John Hay to negotiate an agreement with the Colombian government for control of a six-mile-wide strip of land across Panama. An agreement was reached whereby the United States would pay Colombia ten million dollars in gold and two hundred fifty thousand dollars annually for the land, which the U.S. would control for one hundred years with an option to renew. However, José Marroquín, the Colombian leader, was reluctant to ratify the agreement. He thought the United States should pay Colombia the forty million dollars it was going to pay the French company for its concession. The impasse dragged on for several months, much to Teddy's frustration.

Other things were moving forward, however. The J. P. Morgan case had made it all the way to the Supreme Court, which ruled that the company of Northern Securities should be dissolved. As a result Teddy won the title of "Trustbuster" and the admiration of most Americans.

Then, as November 1903 approached, the impasse over the canal began to break loose. The people of Panama had always had a yearning for independence from Colombia, and over the years they had initiated a string of unsuccessful uprisings. People in Panama were now once again restless. With some encouragement from representatives of the French company, who stood to make a lot of money if they could sell their concession, the Panamanians staged a revolution on the night of November 3 and the following day declared Panama's independence from Colombia. The United States quickly recognized Panama and entered into negotiations with the new government for control of the strip of land necessary to build the canal. Fifteen days after the coup the Hay-Bunau-Varilla Treaty was signed between the United States and Panama. In it Panama gave the United States in perpetuity the use, occupancy, and control of a ten-mile-wide strip of land across the country. Teddy was delighted by the outcome, and work began on the canal in 1904.

That same year was also a presidential election year. As Teddy thought about the election, he came up with the slogan "A Square Deal" to describe his politics. The slogan was meant to convey the idea that government should make sure that both government and businesses ran fairly and without corruption and that all people—business leaders, farmers, laborers, and consumers—had a right to be treated justly.

Such an idea appealed to just about everyone, and Teddy had no difficulty in becoming the Republican nominee for the presidential election of 1904. He was excited about the campaign because it would end the era of being an "accidental" president and allow him to be voted into the position under his own banner.

Teddy chose Charles W. Fairbanks to be his running mate, and the pair won the election by a wide margin. When the results were announced, a group of reporters asked Teddy if he was ever likely to run for president again. Teddy believed that a president should serve only two terms, and so he announced, "Under no circumstances will I be a candidate for or accept another nomination." The reporters scribbled the comment down in their notebooks and transferred it to numerous newspaper stories that circulated around the nation.

This time the swearing-in session was a grand occasion. It was made even more meaningful when Secretary of State John Hay gave Teddy a ring containing a lock of President Lincoln's hair. As a young man, Hay had cut the lock from the dead president's head. The gesture meant a lot to Teddy, and every time he looked at the ring, it reminded him that he was following in the footsteps of a great man in this office.

Chapter 16

Bull Moose

At the start of Teddy's second term in office, world events began to dominate the news, in particular the situation between Japan and Russia. Russian troops had advanced into Manchuria, China, and Korea and were asserting their influence there. This situation greatly perplexed the Japanese, who saw Korea as falling under their sphere of influence. In February 1904 the Japanese had unleashed a devastating attack on the Russian fleet. Over the next year, the Japanese had launched several more successful attacks against the Russians in Manchuria. But the battles had left the Japanese weary and the Russians humiliated, and both sides had been looking for a way out of their conflict.

Teddy had also begun to worry about the conflict, and while he admired the Japanese military strategy in the battles they fought, he fretted that the Japanese might become too strong and interfere with the United States' interests in the Pacific, particularly Hawaii and the Philippines. He called a peace conference between Russia and Japan that was held at the Portsmouth navy yard in New Hampshire in August 1905. At first the two sides were unwilling to compromise. Teddy encouraged them behind the scenes to do so, putting equal pressure on both delegations. Eventually, on the last day of the conference, the two sides broke their impasse and a peace treaty was agreed to and signed. Teddy was delighted by the outcome.

Even as he was dealing with the Russians and the Japanese, Teddy took the time to stay keenly aware of what was happening in the area of conservation. He named James Garfield, a champion of the conservation movement, as his Secretary of the Interior. He also organized the Forest Service so that forestry, mineral, and grazing rights, especially in the western states, would be protected.

While all of this was playing out on the political stage, Teddy's family life continued to be as interesting as ever. His niece Eleanor, his brother Elliot's oldest daughter, was in love with Franklin Roosevelt. Franklin was the only son of Sarah and James Roosevelt, Elliot and Teddy's distant cousin. Elliot had been Franklin's godfather, and Teddy was delighted with the match, especially when the pair decided to marry and he was asked to stand in for the bride's father. The wedding was held on St. Patrick's Day, March 17, 1905.

Less than a year later Alice married a Republican congressman from Ohio named Nicholas Longworth. Nicholas was fifteen years older than Alice, but Alice was convinced that they were a good match. Edith was not so sure. She told Teddy she thought Nicholas drank too much, but Teddy disagreed. On February 17, 1906, Alice and Nicholas Longworth were married in the East Room of the White House. It was the social event of the year in Washington, with over five hundred prominent guests in attendance. Thousands of people gathered outside the White House gates as well, hoping to catch a glimpse of "Princess Alice" on her wedding day.

Six months later a problem developed hundreds of miles away. On August 13, 1906, an unidentified group of between ten and twenty people shot up the small border town of Brownsville, Texas. One citizen was killed and several others injured in the melee. The white people in the town accused the three black army units in the area of carrying out the rampage, while several white military men insisted that the whites had staged the attack to stir up trouble. The army conducted a very fast and superficial inquiry, in which it concluded that the black soldiers had shot up the town. Teddy was incensed, not because the men were black but because as members of the United States military, all soldiers were supposed to stand for law and order. When no one came forward to confess to the act, Teddy ordered that all three companies, totaling 167 men, be dishonorably discharged.

This action caused an uproar, and many people called for a thorough investigation of the incident. But since Teddy felt that the honor of the armed forces was at stake, he refused to order one. Instead he took a trip to Panama to see how work on the canal was progressing.

When he arrived back from his trip to Panama, Teddy had another matter to deal with, again involving the Japanese. Although they were grateful for the peace treaty that had averted all-out war with Russia, the Japanese were bitter because they had not received all they were promised in the peace negotiations. People on the West Coast of the United States began to worry about the Japanese attitude. They fretted that the Japanese might attack them, since the United States had been instrumental in negotiating the peace treaty. This fear, whether real or not, turned to anger against the Japanese-Americans living in California. In October, just before Teddy left for Panama, the San Francisco Board of Education ordered that all Japanese children be removed from their schools and placed in separate, segregated schools. Teddy was outraged by the school board's action, and even more so when he learned that the move had caused widespread rioting in Japan. When he arrived back in Washington from Panama, Teddy fumed about the stupidity of the board of education and wondered aloud if it was deliberately trying to provoke a war.

For tense situations such as these, the United States had been actively seeking to better understand the Japanese mind and military. In the wake of the Russo-Japanese War and the Treaty of Portsmouth, Major General Arthur MacArthur and his son First Lieutenant Douglas MacArthur had traveled twenty thousand miles in the Orient, including in Japan, inspecting hundreds of troops and bases and talking to every available military leader and government official. Teddy had appointed the younger MacArthur as an aide-de-camp to the president, asking his advice on matters pertaining to the Far East.

But Teddy didn't require a Far East expert to conclude that the school board's order to segregate the San Francisco schools was dangerously shortsighted. Enraged, he swung into action. Although the federal government had no control over a school board, Teddy invited all of the San Francisco Board of Education members to the White House and made it very clear to them what he thought. The board quickly backed down and reversed its decision, but Teddy felt that the Japanese had been so insulted that they might still attack the United States.

To remedy this situation, Teddy decided on a show of force. He ordered the American fleet, consisting of sixteen battleships, numerous support craft, and eighteen thousand men, to sail from the East Coast around Cape Horn and into the Pacific Ocean for naval maneuvers. Teddy stood proudly as the ships sailed by him, their flags flying and cannons booming. It was the greatest display of naval strength ever shown in America, and the press soon dubbed it the "Great White Fleet."

By the time the fleet reached San Francisco, the Japanese had softened their stance and invited the ships to visit Yokohama. Teddy was pleased with this outcome and felt that the show of American force had preserved peace in the Pacific.

Meanwhile Teddy was being pressed by the Republicans to run again for president. However, he had stated publicly that he would not run again under any circumstances, and he felt he could not go back on his word. After some debate, he decided to back Secretary of War William Taft as the Republican candidate. Taft was more of a follower than a leader, but Teddy felt confident that the man would carry on the policies he had begun in his seven-and-one-half-year term as president. With Teddy's backing, William Taft won the Republican nomination and then the election of 1908. The Roosevelt era in Washington was over.

Teddy could hardly compose himself as he packed up his belongings and left the White House. He was sure that nothing that he could do in the future would ever rival being president of the United States. At fifty years of age, he felt that the best years of his life were behind him.

After leaving Washington Teddy decided he needed a complete change of pace and, to give William Taft a fair chance at being an effective leader, he had to get out of the United States. Never one to do things on a small scale, Teddy settled on a year-long expedition to Africa!

On April 24, 1909, former President Teddy Roosevelt stood at Kapiti Station in East Africa surveying the scene. In front of him were 15 African soldiers, 260 porters, his son Kermit, and a group from the Smithsonian Museum. Although Teddy hoped to shoot many wild animals, he had a larger purpose in mind. He wanted to preserve the animals he shot and give them to the Smithsonian Institution.

It was one of the largest safaris ever assembled in East Africa, and it set out onto the Kapiti Plains. The plan was to be gone about a year and collect as wide a variety of animals as possible. The hunters were not disappointed. Between them, Teddy and Kermit killed seventeen lions, eleven elephants, forty-seven gazelles, nine giraffes, eight hippopotamuses, nine hyenas, and twenty-nine zebras. Each carcass was quickly skinned and the meat cut off the bones. The skin and bones were processed with portions of the four tons of salt they had brought along for the purpose. Then they were labeled and boxed up for the trip back to Washington, while the meat was prepared and eaten by the men.

Every once in a while the safari camped on the outskirts of Nairobi to buy more supplies. Teddy used the opportunity to send off reports to a publisher who had contracted with him to write a series of articles on the progress of his safari. Teddy collected the mail there as well and found himself grimacing at some of the newspaper reports friends sent him. The ones that worried him most were about President Taft. From what Teddy could read, it appeared that the new president was weak and unable to deal with the growing rift between the conservative and progressive wings of the Republican party. By sheer weight of his personality, Teddy had managed to swing things toward the progressive side when he was president, but William Taft was nowhere near as imposing as Teddy, and he seemed to be bandied about between the two wings.

The year-long safari was nearly over when Edith and Ethel traveled to Khartoum to meet Teddy and Kermit. It was a joyous reunion, especially since Edith brought news of Ted's engagement. Their oldest son's bride-to-be was a woman named Eleanor Alexander.

Teddy was sad when the safari finally ended. He doubted that he would ever again have such an adventurous opportunity. Still, after he had supervised the last dispatch of elephant bones, he said farewell to his fellow travelers and set off across North Africa with his wife and two of his children. They took a nostalgic trip down the Nile River, where Teddy recalled the great adventure he'd had as a boy on the Roosevelt family's trip down the Nile thirty-eight years earlier. Then from Egypt it was on to Italy and several other European countries, including Austria, Hungary, and Holland.

When the day came to go to Oslo, Norway, it was far more than just another stop on their tour. There the family attended a ceremony in which Teddy was awarded the Nobel Peace Prize. It was a proud and historic moment for Teddy and for the United States. Teddy had been selected for the prize for his efforts in keeping Japan and Russia from engaging in all-out war with each other. Being the first American ever to receive such an honor meant a great deal to Teddy.

Even on this trip, Teddy found he was still in public service. When King Edward VII of England died unexpectedly, President Taft telegraphed Teddy and asked him to be the United States' official representative at the funeral, so the family made a detour to London.

When the four Roosevelts returned to New York on June 18, 1910, they received a huge welcome at the dock. Far from being forgotten, the articles Teddy had written during his time in Africa had made him a larger-than-life figure to many Americans.

A week later, Ted and Eleanor were married, bringing the whole Roosevelt family together once again. As Teddy surveyed his sons and daughters, he sensed it would be a long time before they would be together again. Ted had already accepted a job in San Francisco. Alice's husband had climbed through the Republican ranks in the House of Representatives. Kermit was off to Harvard, and at nearly nineteen, Ethel was finding her way in high society, while the two younger boys, Archie and Quentin, were both settled into boarding school.

Once the wedding was over, Teddy and Edith returned to Sagamore Hill, where Teddy began writing a book about his African adventure. Many visitors came to the house to stay for a day or a week, and Teddy regaled them all with safari stories. Some of these visitors were Republican senators and members of the House of Representatives, and Teddy quizzed them about what was really happening in Washington. The more Teddy heard, the more incensed he became. It seemed to him that William Taft was even less effective than he had thought. "I am sure he means well, but he means well feebly, and he does not know how! He is utterly unfit for leadership, and this is a time when we need leadership!" he boomed at one senator. "All kinds of people influence him on the unimportant things where he does know his own mind but generally makes up his mind wrong; and on the important things, he does not know his own mind and changes it every which way."

Teddy had to admit he had done the wrong thing in nominating Taft for president, and now as the 1912 election approached, he was faced with what, if anything, he should do about it. In the end he changed his mind about serving another term as president and decided that if the Republican party nominated him, he would run for president once again. The press criticized him for going back on his promise to serve only two terms, but Teddy felt that the crisis in the Republican party was such that he had to do something.

The Republican party was at war with itself. Half of the party wanted William Taft to be their candidate for president, and the other half wanted Teddy Roosevelt to return to office. Teddy, having thrown his hat into the race, campaigned as vigorously as he ever had.

At the Republican convention in August 1912, Teddy lost the party nomination to William Taft, but he was so energized by the fight that he was not ready to give up. A new party was on the scene, named the Progressive party, which was made up mainly of disgruntled liberal Republicans. Its emblem was the bull moose. Teddy decided to try for the party's nomination for president. The party gladly accepted him, and Teddy ran his second presidential campaign, this time not as a Republican but as a Progressive. He would do his best against William Taft and Woodrow Wilson, the Democrats' choice as their presidential candidate.

As was to be expected, this decision made Teddy many enemies as well as supporters. One enemy was a man named John F. Schrank. Teddy was in Milwaukee, Wisconsin, on October 14, 1912, to make a campaign speech. On the way to give the speech, he stood to acknowledge the cheering crowd. As he did so, Schrank, a local bartender, pulled out a pistol, stepped forward, and shot Teddy in the chest. Teddy reeled backward while the crowd descended on Schrank. Shaken, Teddy stumbled to his feet. He reached inside his overcoat and could feel that he was bleeding. He then held his hand up to his opened mouth and coughed. When he saw that he was not coughing up blood, he decided the wound was not fatal.

Turning to the crowd that was beating Schrank, Teddy said, "Don't hurt him; bring him to me." Teddy gave his would-be assassin a glare of contempt before the police carted him away. Turning to his aides, Teddy told them, "You get me to that speech. It may be the last one I shall deliver, and I am going to deliver this myself."

His startled aides, who wanted him to go straight to the hospital, gave in and guided him to the meeting hall.

Bleeding, Teddy stood to address the crowd. "Friends, I should ask you to be as quiet as possible," he began. "I don't know if you fully understand that I have been shot, but it takes more than that to kill a bull moose."

The crowd went suddenly silent at the revelation, and while getting progressively weaker from the loss of blood, Teddy went on to address them for the next hour and a half. Following the speech his aides took Teddy straight to the hospital for medical attention. There a doctor removed the bullet that was lodged between his ribs.

The presidential election in November was not close. Democrat Woodrow Wilson won. Teddy, recuperating from his gunshot wound, came in second, and William Taft third. Bitter words were soon traded as loyal Republicans pointed out that if the votes cast for Teddy and William Taft were combined, a Republican would still be in the White House.

Teddy was unapologetic. He wrote to Kermit, "Well we have gone down to a smashing defeat....In one sense, of course, this is bad for my reputation, for it rather diminishes the sum of my achievement, which is the only heritage I leave you children. After one has been conqueror it is never pleasing to have a second installment of one's career as a leader of lost causes. On the other hand I do not sincerely feel that there was ever a cause so well worth fighting for as the cause of ours this year."

After the election, back at Sagamore Hill, Teddy was unsure of where his future lay.

Chapter 17

An American Original

Eleven months after the election, Teddy was aboard the *Vandyck* bound for Brazil. Immediately after the election, the Progressive party had begun to disintegrate, and despite his best efforts, Teddy had been unable to resolve the issues affecting the party. Now he needed a break. The plan was for Edith to accompany him on a speaking tour of Brazil, and then he and Kermit would go on some kind of Amazon adventure. Teddy wasn't yet quite sure what that would be, though he hoped it would involve exploring some uncharted rivers.

The Roosevelts spent six weeks speaking around the country, and then Edith returned home in time for Christmas. Before they had left the United States, Ethel had married Dr. Dick Derby, and Edith was eager to get home and spend time with them. It would be only the second time in their married lives that Teddy and Edith had been apart at Christmas.

On the speaking tour, Brazil's minister of foreign affairs had told Teddy about the explorations of Colonel Enrique da Silva Rondon in the headwaters of the unexplored Rio da Divuda, or the River of Doubt. It sounded like just the kind of place that Teddy had in mind for his Amazon adventure. Soon an expedition down the uncharted river was organized, with Colonel Rondon going along as guide and the Brazilian government representative.

On February 27, 1914, after two months of planning, the expedition set out on the River of Doubt and began paddling dugout canoes downstream. Traveling along with Teddy, Kermit, and Colonel Rondon was naturalist George Cherrie. Also going with them were a number of native boatmen. They carried with them food and supplies to last them fifty days. The food and supplies were spread evenly among the various dugout canoes.

Dense jungle crowded in on either side of the river and arched over the river above them. Choking vines hung from the trees, and the air was filled with a cacophony of bird song, crocking, whooshing, and other animal sounds.

For the first three days the river ran wide and fairly straight, but on the fourth day it began to narrow and twist and turn back on itself, and the current began to get stronger. Then the men began to hear a roar in the distance. The roaring got louder and louder, until they rounded a bend and were confronted with thunderous rapids. They paddled the dugouts ashore and explored on foot. The rapids went on for over a mile. At one point the water from the river was forced into a churning gorge between the rocks no more than four feet wide. They would have to portage their canoes around the rapids.

The portage was backbreaking and arduous and took three days to complete, but finally they were able to put their canoes back in the water and head on downstream. However, they had spent only a day and a half back on the river when they came to more rapids and were forced to make a four-day portage around them. Soon they found themselves on the river for only several hours at a time before they would have to pull their canoes out and portage once again. Their progress became agonizingly slow.

On March 11, two of the dugout canoes were swamped and sank, taking with them the food and supplies loaded inside them. The expedition stopped at the river's edge, where the boatmen cut down two trees and made two new dugouts to replace the two that sank, and off they headed again.

Three days later Kermit and his boatman got caught in a swift eddy that swept them over a waterfall. The canoe was smashed on the rocks below, and Kermit was thrown into a seething cauldron of water at the bottom of the waterfall. His wet clothes began to drag him under. Teddy watched helplessly from above as his son struggled to stay alive. Thankfully, with incredible effort, Kermit was able to grab a branch of a tree above the water and slowly inch himself to safety.

The body of Kermit's boatman never surfaced after the mishap, and everything in the canoe was lost, including the Winchester rifle Kermit prized so much and which he had carried with him in Africa on safari.

The expedition continued on down the River of Doubt, but the next day they were forced to portage yet again. It was during this portage that they became aware of another menace they had not accounted for. As they walked along, Colonel Rondon's dog yelped and fell over dead. A poisoned arrow had pierced its heart. Now the expedition had to watch out for unfriendly natives, and from then on they posted a guard each night to watch over their camp.

On March 19, as they continued on downriver, they discovered a large tributary that flowed into the River of Doubt. As the representative of the Brazilian government, Colonel Rondon named it the Rio Kermit, much to Teddy's delight.

Delighted as he was by the gesture, Teddy was becoming dismayed at the way the expedition was going. He had not anticipated so many rapids and having to make so many portages. As a result their food supplies were dropping rapidly. They had traveled for eighteen days and used one-third of their food supplies, but they had covered only one-fifth of the distance they needed to cover. But there was no going back upstream. Teddy knew that their only hope was to keep moving forward, despite the fact that a number of the boatmen had become ill.

One of the dugouts threatened to capsize on March 27, and as Teddy raced into the river to steady it, he gashed his leg on a jagged rock. By nightfall the wound had become infected and was beginning to ooze. The infection continued to spread, despite having a tube inserted into it to drain it.

More rapids and more long portages followed, during which Teddy found it hard to walk. To make matters worse, Teddy had contracted malaria, and soon his fever was so high that he began to slide into periods of delirium.

On the night of March 31, Teddy sat with his back against a tree in driving rain, reciting poetry. He could feel himself fading in and out of consciousness. Kermit walked over and sat beside him.

Teddy was aware of what was going on around him, and he knew he had to get the words out before he became delirious again. "I realize that some of us are not going to finish this journey," he told Kermit. "I know that I am a burden to the rest of you. I will stop here. I need to talk to George Cherrie about the best way to end my life."

Kermit would have none of it. "You will have to keep going," he told his father, "for while you have lost weight on this trip, you are still too heavy for me to pick up and carry. I am determined to bring you back alive."

Teddy smiled at his son. They shared the same stubborn traits.

The following morning Teddy was still alive and felt a little stronger. They ate their ration of food, a cup of coffee and a soda cracker, which they supplemented in the evenings with a few mouthfuls of monkey stew.

The pattern of rapids and portages continued for several more days. Slowly they began to notice that the river was widening out again and the rapids were becoming less frequent.

April 15 Teddy declared a "red letter day." That was the day they discovered a stake driven into the riverbank with initials carved into it. The stake marked out the territory of a rubber gatherer. Finally they were approaching civilization. Then a little farther on they came upon an uninhabited cabin by the river. Teddy felt his spirits begin to soar. Perhaps he was not going to die on the river after all.

Finally the River of Doubt flowed into the Aripunta, which in turn flowed into the Madeira, which emptied into the Amazon, which carried them to civilization, where they arrived sick and weak but alive—and the first people to explore the length of the River of Doubt.

Teddy made it back to the United States, but he was thirty-five pounds lighter, and he felt at least ten years older. He still had malaria, and his leg was not completely healed from the infection. All of his belongings lay at the bottom of the River of Doubt, except for the manuscript he had written along the way titled *Through the Brazilian Wilderness*.

When he arrived by boat at Oyster Bay, Ethel came running to meet him. In her arms was her newborn son, Richard. Tears came to Teddy's eyes as he held his first grandson.

Other family events soon followed. Kermit, who had been engaged for some time to Belle, the daughter of the U.S. Ambassador to Spain, decided it was time to marry. The entire family traveled to Madrid for the wedding, which in itself created quite a diplomatic problem. Spanish Queen Maria Christiana was so incensed that Teddy Roosevelt, the Rough Rider who had helped oust the Spanish from Cuba, was in the country that she left for Vienna.

Christmas 1914 followed. Kermit took a job in Brazil, so he and Belle were unable to be at Sagamore Hill, but the other children all rallied around their parents. Ted and Eleanor had two children by now: a daughter named Grace and a newborn son, Theodore III. But even with his family around him, Teddy could not shake off the ominous feelings about the future. Following the assassination of Archduke Ferdinand in Sarajevo, halfway around the world, Europe had fallen into a major confrontation. Germany was at war with France and England in the west, and Turkey was advancing in the east.

Soon after Christmas, Ethel and her doctor husband volunteered to go to France, where they helped set up a mobile surgical unit. Ethel sent home regular reports to Teddy on what was happening on the battlefront in France.

For his part, Teddy was becoming increasingly disgusted with President Woodrow Wilson for the way he refused to become involved in the Great War in Europe. Instead of sending American troops and arms, Wilson sent off official notes of protest to Germany about what it was doing to other countries. When the Germans sank the passenger liner *Lusitania* on May 7, 1915, Teddy was outraged. Surely now, he argued, President Wilson had to do something, especially since there had been so many Americans aboard the ship. But the president merely sent another letter of protest on behalf of the United States. Eventually, in early April 1917, President Wilson's patience ran out, and he asked Congress to declare war against Germany "to make the world safe for democracy." On April 6 war was declared.

Thoughts of his gallant days as a Rough Rider flooded Teddy's mind, and he decided to relive them. He dreamed of his own cavalry unit, comprising his four sons and the sons of the other Rough Riders. Having dreamed of the glory that lay ahead for such a unit, Teddy did everything he could to pressure the government into allowing him to set it up. But when his plan was stopped at the lower echelons of government, he appealed directly to recently reelected President Wilson. The telegram from the White House declining the offer dashed Teddy's hopes for good of starting such a unit.

Just as the United States declared war on Germany, Archie married Grace Lockwood, a young woman from a good family in Boston. Ethel and Dick came home from France for the wedding, and the whole family was again assembled in one place.

A month later, in early June, Archie and Ted sailed for France to join in the fighting. Ted's wife, Eleanor, sailed soon afterward. She was determined to help in the war effort and signed up to work with the YMCA, even though it meant leaving her three young children at home with her mother. At first Teddy was appalled by her decision, but then he came to see it as a heroic act.

Kermit was the next to go off to war, leaving for the front in early July. His wife, Belle, and their son, Kermit Jr., went as well. Belle had decided to spend the duration of the war in Madrid, Spain, with her parents.

Ethel's husband, Dick, returned to France, and in August, Quentin shipped out for France as a pilot with the U.S. Signal Corps. Now all four sons, one son-in-law, and two daughters-in-law were in Europe. Teddy put a flag with five gold stars in the bay window at Sagamore Hill, symbolizing the five men in their family in service, and then he and Edith waited.

Letters flowed home from the boys, giving Teddy a tantalizing peek at what was happening at the battlefront. Kermit was learning to drive a light armored motorized car, which was really a Rolls-Royce with plate armor and machine guns mounted on the hood. Ted was made commander of the First Battalion of the Twenty-Sixth Infantry. Archie complained of leading a raid against the Germans for which his unit had been issued new boots. His were three sizes too small and cramped his feet so much that he got infected sores on all of his toes. Quentin was given the job of driving a motorcycle around the French countryside, scrounging spare parts to keep Allied airplanes in the air.

Before long Archie was seriously wounded when a German bomb sprayed him with shrapnel. He was sent to Paris to recuperate. Then on July 22, 1918, Teddy received terrible news. Quentin, his and Edith's youngest son, had been shot down and killed behind enemy lines. Teddy's official statement about his son's death read, "Quentin's mother and I are very glad that he got to the front and had a chance to render some service to his country and show the stuff he was made of."

Privately Teddy and Edith grieved together for their son who would never come home and spend another summer with them at Sagamore Hill.

Less than a week later Ted was hit in the leg by machine-gun fire. Two bullets had shattered his knee, and Teddy learned that Ted would probably lose the leg. In addition, Archie's wounds were not healing very well, and he was ordered back to the United States.

At Sagamore Hill the Roosevelts braced themselves for more bad news. They were grateful that it did not come, and Germany surrendered on November 11, 1918. The Great War was over. That same day Teddy had a particularly bad bout of rheumatism. He was in such pain that he agreed to be admitted to Roosevelt Hospital overnight. This was the hospital his father had helped found over fifty years before.

Teddy's one-night stay in the hospital turned into forty-four nights, and Teddy was finally discharged on Christmas Day. His presence at Sagamore Hill lifted the gloom over Quentin's death a little, but everyone had to make him or herself smile at the usual round of family jokes and stories.

Teddy Roosevelt spent Saturday, January 4, 1919, in bed. Early the following morning, his faithful friend, James Amos, who had come to take care of him after his release from the hospital, discovered that Teddy had stopped breathing. Teddy had apparently died from an aneurysm in his heart. He was sixty years old.

"The old lion is dead," Archie telegraphed to Kermit and Ted. Vice President Thomas Marshall remarked of Teddy, "Death had to take him sleeping, for if Roosevelt had been awake, there would have been a fight."

A funeral service was held at the local church in Oyster Bay, and Teddy was laid to rest on a hill overlooking Sagamore Hill.

Soon after he died, Teddy's last book was published. In it was the passage, "Only those are fit to live who do not fear to die. And none are fit to die who have shrunk from the joy of life and the duty of life. Both life and death are parts of the same Great Adventure."

What an adventure it had been for Teddy Roosevelt, a true American original.

Bibliography

Brands, H. W. *TR: The Last Romantic.* Basic Books, 1997.

Collier, Peter. *The Roosevelts: An American Saga.* Touchstone Books, 1994.

McCullough, David. *Mornings on Horseback.* Simon & Schuster, 1981.

Miller, Nathan. *Theodore Roosevelt: A Life.* Quill William Morrow, 1992.

Morris, Edmund. *The Rise of Theodore Roosevelt.* The Modern Library, 1979.

Morris, Edmund. *Theodore Rex.* Random House, 2001.

Roosevelt, Theodore. *An Autobiography.* Da Capo Press, 1985

About the Authors

Janet and Geoff Benge are a husband and wife writing team with more than thirty years of writing experience. Janet is a former elementary school teacher. Geoff holds a degree in history. Originally from New Zealand, the Benges spent ten years serving with Youth With A Mission. They have two daughters, Laura and Shannon, and an adopted son, Lito. They make their home in the Orlando, Florida, area.

Also from Janet and Geoff Benge...

More adventure-filled biographies for ages 10 to 100!

Gladys Aylward: The Adventure of a Lifetime • 978-1-57658-019-6
Nate Saint: On a Wing and a Prayer • 978-1-57658-017-2
Hudson Taylor: Deep in the Heart of China • 978-1-57658-016-5
Amy Carmichael: Rescuer of Precious Gems • 978-1-57658-018-9
Eric Liddell: Something Greater Than Gold • 978-1-57658-137-7
Corrie ten Boom: Keeper of the Angels' Den • 978-1-57658-136-0
William Carey: Obliged to Go • 978-1-57658-147-6
George Müller: Guardian of Bristol's Orphans • 978-1-57658-145-2
Jim Elliot: One Great Purpose • 978-1-57658-146-9
Mary Slessor: Forward into Calabar • 978-1-57658-148-3
David Livingstone: Africa's Trailblazer • 978-1-57658-153-7
Betty Greene: Wings to Serve • 978-1-57658-152-0
Adoniram Judson: Bound for Burma • 978-1-57658-161-2
Cameron Townsend: Good News in Every Language • 978-1-57658-164-3
Jonathan Goforth: An Open Door in China • 978-1-57658-174-2
Lottie Moon: Giving Her All for China • 978-1-57658-188-9
John Williams: Messenger of Peace • 978-1-57658-256-5
William Booth: Soup, Soap, and Salvation • 978-1-57658-258-9
Rowland Bingham: Into Africa's Interior • 978-1-57658-282-4
Ida Scudder: Healing Bodies, Touching Hearts • 978-1-57658-285-5
Wilfred Grenfell: Fisher of Men • 978-1-57658-292-3
Lillian Trasher: The Greatest Wonder in Egypt • 978-1-57658-305-0
Loren Cunningham: Into All the World • 978-1-57658-199-5
Florence Young: Mission Accomplished • 978-1-57658-313-5
Sundar Singh: Footprints Over the Mountains • 978-1-57658-318-0
C.T. Studd: No Retreat • 978-1-57658-288-6
Rachel Saint: A Star in the Jungle • 978-1-57658-337-1
Brother Andrew: God's Secret Agent • 978-1-57658-355-5
Clarence Jones: Mr. Radio • 978-1-57658-343-2
Count Zinzendorf: Firstfruit • 978-1-57658-262-6
John Wesley: The World His Parish • 978-1-57658-382-1
C. S. Lewis: Master Storyteller • 978-1-57658-385-2
David Bussau: Facing the World Head-on • 978-1-57658-415-6
Jacob DeShazer: Forgive Your Enemies • 978-1-57658-475-0

Isobel Kuhn: On the Roof of the World • 978-1-57658-497-2
Elisabeth Elliot: Joyful Surrender • 978-1-57658-513-9
D. L. Moody: Bringing Souls to Christ • 978-1-57658-552-8
Paul Brand: Helping Hands • 978-1-57658-536-8
Dietrich Bonhoeffer: In the Midst of Wickedness • 978-1-57658-713-3
Francis Asbury: Circuit Rider • 978-1-57658-737-9
Samuel Zwemer: The Burden of Arabia • 978-1-57658-738-6
Klaus-Dieter John: Hope in the Land of the Incas • 978-1-57658-826-2
Mildred Cable: Through the Jade Gate • 978-1-57658-886-4
John Flynn: Into the Never Never • 978-1-57658-898-7
Richard Wurmbrand: Love Your Enemies • 978-1-57658-987-8
Charles Mulli: We Are Family • 978-1-57658-894-9
John Newton: Change of Heart • 978-1-57658-909-0
Helen Roseveare: Mama Luka • 978-1-57658-910-6
Norman Grubb: Mission Builder • 978-1-57658-915-1
Albert Schweitzer: Le Grand Docteur • 978-1-57658-961-8
Frederick Douglass: The Right to dignity • 978-1-62486-151-2

Available in paperback, e-book, and audiobook formats.

HEROES OF HISTORY
GEORGE WASHINGTON
True Patriot
JANET & GEOFF BENGE
HARRIET TUBMAN
Freedombound
AUDIO HEROES
Emerald Books